**About the A**

In 1975, Raymond Moody MD, PhD coined the term near-death experience in his book *Life After Life*. For half a century, he has researched some of life's greatest mysteries. As both a PhD in philosophy and an MD, he has had a strong interest in how medical realities intersect with the ineffable realm of philosophy.

Throughout his five-decade career, he has explored themes related to the transpersonal aspects of death, dying and grief. In his book *Glimpses of Eternity*, he discusses the phenomena of shared-death experiences. He writes about his inquiry into past lives in his book *Coming Back* and shares methods for evoking the dead, from Ancient Greece to modern times, in his book *Reunions*.

For more information about Dr. Moody, his books, presentations, future releases and webinars, please visit:

**www.lifeafterlife.com**

*God is Bigger*

*Than the Bible*

**ISBN:** 9798719383743

**Imprint:** *Life After Life* Institute

Raymond Moody MD, PhD

# God is Bigger
# Than the Bible

*We are God's Stories*

*Could we with ink the ocean fill;*

*were the whole earth of parchment made;*

*were every single stick a quill;*

*were every man a scribe by trade;*

*to write the love of God alone,*

*would drain the ocean dry;*

*nor would the scroll contain the whole,*

*though stretched from sky to sky.*

*-- Anonymous, 1799*

# INTRODUCTION

In the spring of 2010, I was sitting on my back porch writing this book when my neighbor Brian came up the steps to get a Coke from the refrigerator. Brian was about 40 years old at the time, but I had known him since he was 17 years old. He worked for us from time to time and he was there that day mowing the grass. So he came up on the porch to sit down and cool off for a few minutes. He looked at what I was doing and asked, "What are you writing, Raymond?"

I said, "I am writing a book called, 'God is Bigger than the Bible'."

Brian's head literally jerked and shock registered on his face. His head bobbed and bowed slightly. He cast his eyes downward and he said, "Huh! Sometimes I think His word is even greater than He is."

Since then, many other fine people had the same strong, startled, surprised reaction to my title. Hearing and contemplating the title leaves them agitated and exasperated. Yet if you think it over for a minute, I believe you will agree with me. God is far, far greater than the Bible.

For God is the Supreme Being, a being greater than which none other can be conceived. To say that a book, the Bible, a written product of human beings is greater than the Supreme Being, Almighty God, makes no intelligible sense. If you will work it out in your own mind, you will see it for yourself.

However divinely inspired and guided the scribes and compilers of the Bible might have been, they are not on a par with God. We can count the exact number of words in the Bible. We can weigh the Bible or measure it with a ruler. No doubt some are able to recite the Bible word for word from beginning to end. Perhaps a few can even recite the Bible backwards, or in seven different languages. But in no way do any such impressive feats or skills enable us to comprehend the greatness upon greatness upon greatness of God. For in reality, God is bigger than the Bible.

Still, it is strange how many people cannot keep God and the Bible clearly separate in their minds. Is fear part of their problem? Some people get scared sick if they have to say, "I don't know."

Rather than conceding that there are many things, including things about God, that they don't know, they concretize God. They try to put God into a box, and they call that box the Bible.

Many people who bluster about the Bible don't really know much about it. If you haven't noticed this already, you will realize it yourself if you question them gently. These people are intrusively assertive about what the Bible supposedly says, but they don't know what they are talking about. In effect, they have become bibliolatrers.

Bibliolatry is worshipping a book. And the Bible is the particular book that many bibliolaters worship. They spend lots of time reading the Bible, pontificating on the Bible and trying to inflict their views about the Bible on other people. The physicality of the Bible often seems part of the mystique it holds for them. They like to wave it about, thump on it or use it like a prop. They don't seem to keep God clearly separate from the Bible in their minds.

Yet, it is perfectly possible to have a good, strong, growing, loving relationship with God without ever reading a single word of the Bible. In fact, plenty of people out there in the world have a good, strong relationship with God, but are largely ignorant of the Bible. I am one of them myself.

When I was a child, my family was not religious. My father was sarcastic about religion. Dad was a military officer and surgeon who served in the Pacific during World War II. His generation was not very talkative about their wartime experiences. Later, I surmised that what Dad experienced during the War must have soured him on religion.

Meanwhile, my maternal grandmother often poked

gentle fun at her religious friends and their foibles. I think that the intolerant side of religious people made my grandmother pretty uncomfortable. When I was 8 years old we had a galvanized tub with two handles. One hot summer day, I filled the tub with water to splash and soak for a little while. I wore my Uncle Fairley's fuzzy navy blue swimming trunks with a white stripe on each side.

When I finished splashing, I left the dripping wet swimming trunks in the tub and dashed into the house a few feet away. My grandmother was genuinely irritated with me. She pointed to the people sitting on the front porch of the house next door. And she snapped, "Raymond, those people are Christians!" From her words and tone of voice, I gathered two things. First, we were not Christians. And, secondly, Christians must be pretty severe, stuffy people.

At that time, astronomy was my favorite pastime. I built my own telescope and loved gazing into the night sky and wondering what other planets might be like. I don't remember thinking or talking or asking about

God. I wouldn't call myself an atheist at that age because I did not have a positive opinion that there is no God. I suppose I was an agnostic, or thought that it is impossible to know that there is or is not a God. I focused on astronomy, not on God, and at age 18 I went to the University of Virginia to study the subject.

I took a course on Plato my first semester and immediately decided to major in philosophy, instead. Reading Plato's *Republic* was the first time I realized that some people take the idea of life after death seriously. Up to then, my sole exposure to the idea was in cartoons in magazines. I thought the drawings of clouds, pearly gates and angels were entirely a joke. But I saw that Plato was serious when he emphasized the importance of the question of an afterlife.

At the end of the *Republic*, Plato recounted a story of a warrior who was apparently killed in battle. However, the warrior revived spontaneously during his funeral. The warrior told the startled spectators that he had left his body and visited another realm during his presumed death. I asked Professor Hammond about the story, and he said that such experiences were well known to early Greek philosophers. The philosophers studied cases of people who reported profound visions when they almost died.

Plato was inclined to accept that the experiences were real. However, some other philosophers discounted them. For instance, the philosopher Democritus had figured out that things in the world are made of minute, invisible bits he called atoms. Democritus explained the experiences of people who survived apparent death in terms of residual biological activity in the body. For there is no such thing as an exact moment of death, Democritus insisted.

That was the first I ever heard of what we now know as near-death experiences. I had no idea then that these experiences are also common in the modern world. However, in 1965, three years later, I met a living person who reported a near-death experience. Dr. George Ritchie was then a professor of psychiatry at the University of Virginia. The experience George had while he was clinically dead changed his life and the lives of many other people, including mine.

In December 1943, George was a recruit in the Army at Camp Barkeley, Texas. George contracted double lobar pneumonia and was pronounced dead for nine minutes. A doctor resuscitated him by injecting adrenaline directly into his heart. George said that when his heart stopped beating he left his body. He found himself in the presence of a being of bright light and complete, loving compassion whom George identified as Christ. Christ guided George through a vivid panoramic review of everything he had ever done in his life.

Dr. Ritchie was very generous and often lectured to student groups. I went to one of his lectures, and it was a turning point in my life. Hearing George that night was the first time I ever consciously felt and experienced the spirit of the divine.

After that night I continued studying philosophy and received my Ph.D. in the subject in 1969. I became a philosophy professor and soon I was hearing accounts of near-death experiences from students and colleagues. In 1972 I went to medical school and received my M.D. in 1976. Afterwards, I served as a resident in psychiatry and eventually worked as a forensic psychiatrist. Throughout my career, I continued to interview people about their near-death experiences. The thousands of people I interviewed shared with me the encounters they had with God as they were out of their bodies, hovering on the edge of death.

God shines through these people's stories as a powerfully loving, compassionate, insightful, humorous, utterly delightful and still deeply mysterious presence. I did not have a religious background and I have read very little of the Bible. This book concerns what I learned about God from people's accounts of their near-death experiences and from my own personal encounters with God.

I am not interested in persuading anyone else of my own views and understanding of God. I offer these thoughts only because I know there are many people out there who are like me. They are looking for God and yet they are not interested in organized religion and they just don't relate to the Bible. I met many such individuals during the fifty years I have been lecturing on near-death experiences. My message to them is that religious people and Bible believers don't have a monopoly on the quest to understand God.

The Bible grew, over centuries, from a culture I revere, a culture that also sprouted relatives and friends I dearly love. Therefore, let me make something completely clear from the beginning. Namely, I am not saying anything bad about the Bible. Instead, I am writing about misuses and abuses of the Bible - or Bible abuse. I think Bible abuse is a kind of spiritual illness and I hope this book helps heal it.

From my studies, I know enough about the Bible to know that I don't know much about the Bible. I understand that a lifetime of in-depth scholarship would be required to scratch the surface of a subject as vast as the Bible. I understand this because of my analogous experience of studying Greek philosophy.

For I have studied that subject assiduously and continually since I was 18 years old - 58 years ago. Yet, there is still far, far more about Greek philosophy that I don't know than I do know. And I can see that the same kind of difficulty would apply to studying the Bible.

Even so, some individuals seriously claim authority on Bible matters because of a religious conversion that happened to them overnight. And I think that kind of behavior scares other people away from enjoying a loving relationship with God. That is an example of what I mean by Bible abuse. For people shouldn't be afraid that God is going to hold it against them that they aren't knowledgeable about the Bible.

I know many fine people who draw genuine spiritual inspiration from the Bible. And they are humble souls who understand their personal limitations. But there are other people who abuse the Bible by using it as a cudgel to try and intimidate others. The Bible is one way to pursue a spiritual quest for a loving relationship with God. But using the Bible to threaten others with damnation or to claim to know things one does not know is Bible abuse. Religious believers may be no more informed on a subject than are you or I. Yet, they think that the Bible gives them a license to act like know-it-alls. Bible abusers like them are not just obnoxious. They are positively dangerous to themselves and others.

I extend that same line of thinking to holy books of other great world religions and spiritual traditions. Consider, for instance, the Koran of Islam and the Upanishads of Hinduism. Some draw on those holy books for genuine spiritual enlightenment while others draw on those same texts to justify terroristic violence. Abuse of holy scriptures pertains not just to the Bible but also to other holy texts.

So to repeat, I am not scoffing at the Bible or any holy book. Reading and studying a holy book is one way of seeking God. And there are other ways, too. You can enjoy a loving relationship with God without dwelling on the Bible or any other holy scriptures.

As I am putting the finishing touches on this book America is in the grip of a terrifying worldwide pandemic. Hundreds of thousands of people have died and millions more are facing unemployment due to the economic fallout from the pandemic. And there is no end in sight.

Many people are seeking God or calling on God with great urgency. People tell me they find it hard to think straight or concentrate during this time of turmoil. Reading can be difficult when you have trouble concentrating. So I present you with this compact book for reading at your own pace. The book is made up of thirteen thoughts about God which occurred to me while listening to wonderful people recount their profound near-death experiences. The chapters are brief, to the point, and self-contained. Each chapter invites you to pause and reflect on what it contains from your own point of view and your own personal life experiences. For we are now caught up in a worldwide social, political, economic, spiritual crisis. I hope this book brings you some comfort and consolation. And may God bless us all in these troubling times.

The first of my thoughts, then, is that God is bigger than the Bible. My second thought goes even further. For I say that God is greater than existence itself.

# CHAPTER ONE

# God and Existence

"Do you believe that God exists?"

People sometimes ask me that question. And when they do, I always reply "No, absolutely not!" Then I explain what I mean.

I, Raymond Moody, am a limited human being. I am beset by a host of weaknesses, faults, deficiencies and failings. Any "belief" I could possibly form about God, the Supreme Being, would be bound to be off base in one direction or another. My "beliefs" are irrelevant to God.

Besides, consider that question again. "Do you believe that God exists?" The emphasis of that sentence falls on the word "exists" rather than on God. We think that by drawing a mental boundary line around God, we can contain and confine God within our human conceptual system. And one of the most common ways of attempting this is saying "God exists." However, the trouble is that God is too great to be captured or enclosed within a concept such as "existence."

Some people get into endless debates with others as to whether or not God "exists." I have known people whose main activity in relationship to God is thinking, talking and arguing about whether or not God exists. Sometimes, I suspect that this activity is actually their way of keeping their distance from God or trying to keep God from getting too close. Better ruminate on abstractions like existence and belief, they may feel, than risk getting up close and personal with the Supreme Being.

I was once a university professor of philosophy. In that capacity, I loved teaching logic and critical thinking. "Existence" is a central concept of one branch of logic. So it would take me about an hour to explain the logical concept of existence and show how to symbolize that concept. But that would not help you or me or anyone else in their personal search for God.

Philosophers have said some interesting and enlightening things about existence. For instance, the great Immanuel Kant (1724-1804) said that existence is not a predicate. That is, saying that a thing exists is not like attributing a specific property to it. J.L. Austin, my favorite twentieth century philosopher, also made an enlightening remark about existence. Austin said, "Existing is not something things do, like breathing, only quieter."

Neither the concept of existence nor its contrasting polar opposite concept of non-existence are serviceable for thinking about the Supreme Being. Of course, this sounds abstruse, and that is my point. I don't approach thinking about God by invoking abstract concepts like existence, non-existence or belief. Instead, I approach thinking about God in terms of my interpersonal relationships. I don't say, "I believe that God exists." Rather, I say, "I have a personal relationship with God." And that brings me to my third thought about God. God participates in our interpersonal relationships.

## CHAPTER TWO

# God and Relationships

I talk with God in prayers every morning and every evening and normally several times during the day. I pray a lot and often inspiring and wonderful things happen in the wake of prayers. That is one part of what I mean by saying that I have a personal relationship with God. And I suspect that God participates, usually as an unnoticed third party, in our relationships with other people. Here is an example of what I mean.

In May of 1990, I moved into an old grist mill. The mill was built in 1839 but it had last been rewired in 1950. I knew it needed electrical work but I didn't have the money to pay for the rewiring at that time.

In September of 1993, my wife Cheryl mentioned to me that we were then able to get the money together to pay for the rewiring. We didn't know an electrician, though. So we stood by our kitchen sink and prayed that God would send us just the right electrician.

The next morning, the phone rang and when Cheryl answered it, a voice on the other end said, "Hello. This is B.R. Wilson."

Cheryl said, "Yes, B.R., what is it?"

And B.R. said, "Well, your number just came up on my beeper."

Cheryl said, "We haven't made any phone calls this morning, B.R. What is this about?"

And B.R. said, "Well I'm an electrician."

So Cheryl said, "We do need an electrician, B.R., so come on over."

Within a short time, B.R. arrived and began his inspection. I was standing at the same spot where

Cheryl and I sent up the prayer, but facing the opposite direction, when I first laid eyes on B.R. He was walking into the kitchen from the dining room and he had a puzzled look on his face. He said, "I sure do wish I knew how your number came up on my beeper."

Without a moment's reflection, I blurted out, "Oh, I'm sure it was God!"

B.R. looked somewhat taken aback, but he didn't comment and he went on with his inspection. When he finished, he walked out onto the porch and I sat down in my rocking chair while Cheryl escorted B.R. to his van. Pretty soon, they came back onto the porch and B.R. was looking somewhat rattled. And Cheryl, who is pale-complexioned anyway, looked as white as the proverbial sheet.

Cheryl explained that as B.R. was getting into his van, he said "It's going to be a few days before I can get out here to do this. I come from a very close family and we all love each other very much. My 38-year-old brother dropped dead of a heart attack the other day and my mother had a heart attack on the way back from the funeral home."

Cheryl said, "My husband might be able to help you with that, B.R. He talks with people who are grieving and going through a tough time."

"Well…" B.R. said, "My mother gave me this book called *Life After Life* to read, and it's helping some."

*Life After Life* is the book I wrote in 1974 to describe my research into people's near-death experiences. And that is an example of what I mean when I say I have a relationship with God.

God participated in my relationship and Cheryl's relationship with B.R. That is certainly how it looks to me. God sent us a good electrician that day, just as we asked. And God sent us a good friend that day, too. That took place twenty-seven years ago as I am writing these words. And B.R. is still our friend.

So, yes, I think God participates in our

relationships with others, though exactly how is mysterious. I also think that how God participates varies from relationship to relationship. Incredible as it may seem, I gather that God somehow participates in some of our relationships before we are born. And I don't mean the kind of relationship we obviously have with our mothers before we are born. For instance, I sense that my relationship with my friend and mentor Dr. George Ritchie somehow got started while I was still in the womb.

Dr. Ritchie was from Richmond, Virginia and my mother and father were from Porterdale, Georgia. As I mentioned earlier, Dr. Ritchie's experience took place at Camp Barkeley, Texas. He was taking basic training as an Army recruit, and his experience happened on December 24, 1943. And as I also mentioned, I got to know him and heard his story in 1965 when I was a philosophy major at the University of Virginia.

I wrote my book *Life After Life* in 1974 when I was in medical school at the Medical College of Georgia. I telephoned Dr. Ritchie in September of that year to ask for his permission to dedicate my book to him. He replied, "Well, that's very nice. But I would prefer you dedicate the book to the Christ who gave me this experience."

That is why the dedication to *Life After Life* reads, "To George Ritchie, M.D., and through him, to the One whom he suggested." That brief phone call was the only contact I had with George since 1965, when I first heard of his experience. *Life After Life* was published in November of 1975 and I graduated from medical school shortly thereafter, in January of 1976.

I applied for a residency in psychiatry at the University of Virginia. So my wife and I traveled to Charlottesville in March of 1976 for my admission interviews. While we were there, I phoned George to say hello. True to his generous nature, he invited us to dinner that night and we had a lively and fascinating conversation.

The next day, my wife and I flew back to Macon, Georgia, where my parents lived. That evening, sitting in their living room, I was talking with my father. I casually mentioned to him that the evening before we had dinner with Dr. Ritchie, the first person I heard describe a near-death experience.

By then, my father had heard a tape recording of Dr. Ritchie relating his experience. And I was taken aback at my father's reaction when I mentioned Dr. Ritchie. A puzzled, reflective, even somewhat stunned expression appeared on Dad's face, and he lapsed into telegraphic speech.

Telegraphic speech is a terse, abbreviated manner of speaking typical of telegrams, where it was used as a cost-saving measure. I knew from my medical training that telegraphic speech is also a sign of anxiety. And because I was so struck by the transformation in Dad's expression and speech, I remember exactly what he said.

Dad said, "Huh! That's really interesting. George Ritchie. Camp Barkeley, Texas. December, 1943. You know, I was there. And so were you!"

Dad explained that he and my mother moved to Camp Barkeley in early September, 1943 so that Dad could go to Officers' Candidate School. I was conceived there in late September. George's experience took place at Christmastime. And my father and mother moved away from Camp Barkeley on December 29, 1943. So I was there in utero when the experience that so shaped my life happened to George.

Now flash back twelve years with me to the summer of 1964. I was riding through a remote rural area in Georgia with my uncle, a law enforcement officer, as he was on patrol. On a long backwoods dirt road we spotted an old gristmill beside a creek and I was instantly transfixed by the building. I thought that this kind of place would be an ideal home. We got out of the car and walked around the mill for a while and then my uncle drove me back home.

For several summers thereafter I drove around throughout rural Georgia looking for old gristmills and talking with their owners. Of course, I was mostly daydreaming for I was penniless. Nonetheless, I was also thinking ahead, wondering if I might someday be in a position to purchase an old gristmill. Reality intruded, though, and in my travels I eventually realized two things. First, old gristmills are few and far between. And secondly, the owners of old gristmills are reluctant to part with them. So I let my fantasy go and I didn't think about it any longer.

Now, flash forward with me more than two decades to November 1989. I was serving as a psychology professor at West Georgia College in Carrollton, Georgia. I had made an intriguing discovery and wanted to conduct further research. The research I envisioned required a facility in a rural setting away from prying eyes. So I had been looking for a building in rural areas around the college. I soon found out, though, that Carrollton was under the sway of the Atlanta real estate market. I couldn't find any suitable place within my means. The kindhearted secretary of the Psychology Department knew about my plight. And when I walked into her office that November day she smiled and gave me a cheerful message.

She and her husband were from Alabama and she said if I looked across the state line, real estate was much less expensive. Alabama was only a few miles away and she assured me I would be able to find an affordable place over there. So I asked my good friend Robin, who was a real estate agent in Atlanta if she would help me look. Robin was originally from Alabama and I figured she would be the right person for the task.

Now, at this point I must digress and interject that I have virtually no sense of direction. I always prefer to stay in one place because unless someone guides me around I invariably get lost in unfamiliar locations. Robin knew this very well. So I specified only three conditions. First, the place had to be in a rural area. Secondly, it needed to be inexpensive. Then, thirdly, it needed to be fairly close to the state line. I was teaching classes at the College three days a week. So I had to travel back and forth to Carrollton easily on those days. I also want to emphasize that I never said anything whatsoever to Robin about old gristmills. I gave up on that aspiration over twenty years earlier and Robin knew nothing about it.

One evening in January of 1990, Robin telephoned me with some news. She asked if she could drive me to Alabama the next morning on a house-hunting expedition. I agreed and she showed up as scheduled, and I got into her car. As she drove she explained that her son's best friend was a deputy sheriff in Alabama. She had contacted the deputy, whose name is Don, for advice. When she did, it happened that Don had read *Life After Life* with interest. So Don was happy to help us by driving us around his county that day. Robin didn't even tell me the name of the county because she understood that that kind of information goes right over my head.

We met Don at a Shoney's restaurant and after lunch we set out on our mission. He drove us around the countryside for about two hours. Then I saw a beautiful little Victorian cottage with a For Sale sign posted in the front yard.

I was interested in seeing it and the real estate agent

listed on the sign - Kirk Moore - was a friend of Don's. So Don drove us to Kirk's office, where I asked him about the Victorian cottage that was for sale. And Kirk, as I guess real estate agents are wont to do, first asked "Well, what are you looking for?"

I explained to Kirk that I was a psychiatrist and psychology professor. I told him I was looking for a place out in the country where I could do some research and writing.

I was standing in Kirk's office when I said this and he was standing with his right side toward me. I saw Kirk's eyes turn upward and he looked as though he were gazing at something far, far away. And he said, "Hmm. Let me take you by a place near where I live."

So he drove us along a remote, winding country road to an old gristmill. Of course, at first I thought I must be dreaming. The whole experience was very surreal. Then, Kirk turned around and started driving back to his office. Kirk said that the elderly couple living there weren't happy with the idea of selling it.

But their children, who went to the same church as Kirk, were worried about their parents living by themselves so far from civilization. So they had enlisted their friend Kirk to help them ease their parents - Captain and Mrs. Doerr - out of the place.

These events took place in the era before cell phones. So Kirk drove all the way back to his office so he could talk to the Doerrs on the telephone. There, in my presence, Kirk made a telephone call and Mrs. Doerr answered. Kirk said, "Mrs. Doerr, I'm with a man from out of town, and I wonder if I could bring him by and let him see your house."

I heard Mrs. Doerr's somewhat cranky and grumpy voice protesting, but she relented and Kirk drove us back to the mill. And when we stepped in the front door I introduced myself as Raymond Moody. Then Mrs. Doerr said, "Raymond Moody. Raymond Moody. Are you the man who wrote that book?"

I said I was, and Mrs. Doerr took me by the hand and led me to a bookcase beside the big fireplace in the living room. There, she reached into the bookcase and drew George Ritchie's book, to which I wrote the foreword, off the shelf. As she did, she opened the book and showed me the warm inscription George had written to the Doerrs. She said, "Dr. George Ritchie is one of our dear, dear friends." Then, after a pause, she said, "This must be a sign."

So that is how I came to live in an old gristmill. As it turned out, George had visited the Doerrs in that very house numerous times. That is where, three and a half years later, I met my friend B.R. And that is another example of what I mean when I say that God participates in our relationships with others.

But why, exactly, is God interested in participating in our interpersonal relationships? To me, the whole matter is deeply mysterious and probably even incomprehensible to us while we are alive on Earth. However, I think there is a clue to answer in the life reviews that occur during people's near-death experiences.

# CHAPTER THREE

# God's Love

Early in my psychiatry residency, I figured out that most people chase something. I saw that some of my patients were chasing power. However, it seemed that it didn't satisfy them once they got it. Others were chasing sex in an endless runaround. Yet others were chasing fame and it seemed that what they were really looking for was self-esteem - feeling better about themselves. They seemed to imagine that if a lot of other people liked and admired them they might like themselves, too. Some of my patients were chasing money. Some got it and others didn't. And at age 76 with two kids, I wish I had chased money, too, at some point earlier in my life. But I was preoccupied with teaching philosophy and learning about medicine and psychiatry.

Anyway, one day I reported my observation to my very wise supervisor. "John, I notice that everybody seems to be chasing something. I'm feeling a little uneasy about myself because I'm not chasing anything. I enjoy what I'm doing now."

John smiled his comforting, understanding smile. "Raymond," he asked, "How old were you when you finished your first doctoral degree, in philosophy?"

"I was twenty-four," I replied.

He went on, "Then, as I remember, you taught philosophy for three years. After that you went to medical school. So how old were you when you finished your second doctoral degree?"

"I was thirty-one years old," I said, and somewhere in mid-sentence I realized that I was chasing knowledge. Yes, I have spent my life chasing knowledge and it has been a satisfying and fulfilling quest for me. For when I was about eight years old I realized that as much as I loved knowledge, I would never have much of it compared to the cosmic scale. Still, the relative paucity of human knowledge somehow enhances the joy that comes from the little of it we can get in this life.

The legions of people I interviewed about their near-death experiences had been chasing all those things, too, before their personal encounters with God. Afterwards, however, whatever they were chasing before, they came to a common understanding. They agreed that what this life seems to be about, in large part, is learning to love.

This understanding is thrust upon them through holographic, panoramic reviews which simultaneously focus on every detail of their earthly lives.

In panoramic life reviews, people view the details of their lives through the lens of love - God's love. Many revisit their lives in the presence of a bright light - a personal being composed of light - or love. In that transcendent state, they say, the light is identical with sheer, indescribable love and compassion. They identify the personal being of light as God, or Christ, or an angel. The identifying word varies from individual to individual depending partly, it seems, on their religious, spiritual or cultural traditions. Even so, whatever identifying term they use, their descriptions converge. They encounter a divine being of light of complete compassion who knows everything about them and loves them totally and completely. Everyone says that the love they felt from the light of God surpassed anything that we experience as love in this life. And the contrast between God's love and love experienced in this world is too great to be described, or put into words.

When I lecture on near-death experiences, people often ask me, "What kind of love are we supposed to be learning to give, while we are living in this world?"

That is a good question. "Love" is not just a descriptive term, it is also a normative,     prescriptive, or evaluative term. When we say we "love" someone or something we are thereby placing a positive value on that person, place or thing. People use the same word, "love", when they say "I love Jane", "I love New York", or "I love pie and ice cream". Because we associate a positive value with "love", it feels good and inspiring when we hear that people who report near-death experiences tell us that the purpose of this life is to learn to love. That certainly gives us something to aspire to in this life. Nevertheless, the word "love" has a wild, wide array of different meanings and uses. So what people with near-death experiences tell us can be confusing, too. What they say is inspiring, but for it to be a practical guide for life, we need more detail. What kind of love, exactly, are they talking about?

Romantic love comes naturally to many people's minds when they hear that word "love." That is the kind of love that we most often see played out on the screen when we go to the movies. Romantic love has been characterized as a religion consisting of two people. "Roman" is a French word for "novel." That contains a clue to what romantic love is. Romantic love has a story attached to it. People who experience romantic love love to tell the story of how they met and got to know each other.

Companionate love is the love that grows between two people through the companionship they share over long stretches of time. Passionate love involves and emphasizes the dimension of motivation, or intense motivation. Commitment is another dimension of love - two people mutually committing themselves to stay together and help each other through thick and thin, through the good times and the bad times.

Storge (a Greek term) is a wondrous form of love that used to be common in America but is vanishing from today's society. When we were largely an agricultural and rural nation, practically everybody knew what storge was. I learned the term when I was an undergraduate philosophy student studying ancient Greek. And I immediately understood it because of instances of it in my own family.

In an earlier, rural America kids from adjacent farms would often grow up together as playmates, friends and companions. Their parents owned farms that were next to each other, so geographical destiny put a boy and a girl together. With nobody else around for miles and miles, they knew each other from birth and got to know each other well. Playmates became friends became lifelong confidantes and companions, long before there were any thoughts of sex. They formed an unbreakable bond before they were even aware of sex. Relationships like that just naturally evolved into committed, companionate marriages.

My Aunt Dwight and Uncle Clifford had exactly that type of marriage. I visited them frequently on their farm when I was a kid and they taught me many, valuable life lessons. But when Uncle Clifford died, that was pretty much the end for Aunt Dwight, too. She was never again the same.

I have been guiding people through grief in my practice for decades. I have come to see that the experience of grief depends partly on what type of love existed between the two people. I think that grief is particularly difficult in cases of storge love. Often, when one of the two people dies, the other follows soon thereafter.

So love is a wonderful, multifaceted, complex thing. Just hearing the word can lift us up, convey joy and even inspire us. We also ought to reflect on the complications and heartbreak that comes from love. The psychologist Erich Fromm once observed that although virtually all of us idealize love in theory very few of us ever get it right in practice.

I have been going on and on about love because of what people with near-death experiences tell us. They said that during their life reviews they discovered that the purpose of this life is to learn to love. But what kind of love do they mean?

To me, life reviews are perhaps the most interesting element of peoples' near-death experiences. After they left their bodies, time came to a standstill and a panorama appeared around them of everything they had done in their life. They experienced every action in review but not just from the perspective they had at the time the action took place. Instead, they also revisited the action from the perspectives of the people with whom they had interacted. Hence, when they reviewed scenes in which they had treated someone else harshly, they directly felt the pain their action had caused. Or in scenes in which they had treated others with loving kindness, they directly and empathically experienced the good feelings their actions had created.

In these reviews, God was aware of every action and prompted the person with a question, though the question was not in words. Rather, God directed a thought to the person. People invariably put the question into words as something like, "How have you learned to love?"

Whatever appeared in the panoramic review, people felt that God loved them for themselves, completely and totally. The situation itself naturally made people want to be that same way. People generally told me that God did not judge them during their experience of the review. God's purpose seemed to be education, not judgement.

Even so, many people told me they judged themselves during their review. God's attitude was that they had been learning. Yet, they felt strong regret and remorse for some incidents. Consciousness of the effects of their misdeeds on others, directly compared to the immense love they felt from God, profoundly affected people. They resolved that henceforward they would endeavor to keep God's love constantly in mind when interacting with others in this world.

Life reviews during near-death experiences are suffused with God's light and love. People with transcendent near-death experiences return with a conviction that learning love is the essential meaning and purpose of life. Yet they often find it difficult to adhere to that standard while living in this world. Even given their vision of the importance of love they still find themselves sometimes snapping at others or behaving in a mean-spirited way. Even my friend George Ritchie, the finest person I ever knew, complained of this problem.

George once said, "Raymond, this experience

makes your humanity even more of a burden, in a way." What George meant was that even after seeing the vital importance of love, we are still human beings. I put George's point more bluntly: Let's face it; it is very difficult to get through the average day without wanting to choke at least one person. And that does not change just because of a life review during a near-death experience.

What does change, however, is someone's underlying motivation. After life reviews during their near-death experiences, people are more strongly motivated to change. They generally become more loving in their daily lives. During my career, I got to know thousands of people with near-death experiences. I think that they do very well in their quests. Many of them recounted to me that after their experiences they occasionally felt a longing or intense nostalgia or homesickness for the love of God.

Life reviews during near-death experiences may well bear on the question of life after death. Setting the afterlife aside, however, what we know about life reviews warrants a startling, mind-bending conclusion. Namely, at least for many of us, life is a two-phase process. First we live life forward as the actor, or protagonist. Then, there is a 180 degree turnaround and time stands still. In that timeless state, we relive everything we did through the eyes and feelings of the other characters in our life. Furthermore, the whole life review is suffused with the bright light of God's love.

That second phase takes place in another framework of reality beyond time and space and in a transcendent state of consciousness. That conclusion certainly seems true although it is startling in its implications. And it shows that God loves us far, far more than we love God. Furthermore, we are not expected to live this life up to the standard of God's great love for us.

In reality, the most satisfying and pleasurable style of life, in the long run, is a life of loving and serving others. First, we may hear that as an ideal. Then, we may entertain it as an aspiration. Finally, at long last, we understand it as an indubitable fact of life experience. And God apparently allows a lot of latitude in the adventures we experience individually on our way toward coming to understand that reality.

I suspect that God's love for us is multidimensional in ways we are not capable of comprehending or even imagining while living this life. God's love has all sorts of manifestations and powers that are beyond the reach of the mind. However, one thing does seem clear and demonstrable. Specifically, God's love for us is somehow tied to our capacity to create, tell and appreciate stories, or narratives.

Story is an aspect of life that firmly links us to God's vast, enduring, incomprehensible love. In large part, a person's life is a story. And I say that we are God's stories.

# CHAPTER FOUR

# God's Stories

God made people, Ellie Wiesel said, because God loves stories. Ellie Wiesel, a deep soulful man, survived Auschwitz to win the Nobel Prize for literature after the war. I am awed by Mr. Wiesel's humanity and presence of mind amidst the horrible ordeals he suffered. His life path led him to realize that God loves watching our life stories.

By contrast, I have led a pampered life. Hence, it is with real humility that I concur with his thought. For I came to that same conclusion by a different path of life.

God loves tuning in to our life stories. From what people say about their life reviews, I gather that God follows every individual's life story as it unfolds.

Furthermore, not only does God watch the nuances of every person's life story, God also watches all those stories weave together through their interconnections. God sees an immense interweaving of life stories that is invisible to any single person. God views the whole in a single sweep. And every person's life story is connected through God's immense store of life reviews to every other person's life story.

Life reviews pertain to an ancient philosophical puzzle known as the problem of personal identity. Around 600 BCE, in Greece, a man, Hermotimus, gained fame for his ability to get out of his body at will. Hermotimus would leave his body and travel to distant locations to see what was happening there. Hence, early Greek philosophers grasped that we consist of minds (or souls) and bodies. So they wanted to figure out which one determines our personal identity. Are we essentially souls or bodies?

Plato eventually propounded the theory that personal identity resides in our immaterial, immortal souls. The physical body, Plato said, is constantly changing and it has no part in stable reality. The body, Plato thought, is a vessel or vehicle of the soul which dissolves when the soul leaves it. In his sterner frame of mind, Plato claimed that the body is a jailhouse or prison of the soul. And he portrayed dying people as joyous escapees, as long as they had led a life of pursuing knowledge as wisdom. Philosophy, Plato said, is a rehearsal for dying.

In the seventeenth century, Plato's theory that personal identity resides in an immaterial soul fell out of favor. Certainly, the notion of an immortal, immaterial soul feels warm and fuzzy to us. Nonetheless, philosophers like Thomas Hobbes (1588-1679) argued that the idea of an immaterial soul is meaningless and incoherent, upon careful analysis. The idea that the immaterial soul is not an intelligible concept took hold in western thought.

Philosopher John Locke (1632-1704) defined personal identity in terms of memory. Locke said that the essence of a person's identity consists of that person's memories. In other words, the self consists of that person's memories.

David Hume (1711-1776) then took a more radical step. He maintained that when he looked most deeply into what he thought of as his self, he never could find any persistent, underlying entity. When he looked within, Hume said, he could find only passing impressions. This view of the self as a mental and linguistic fiction, or illusion, is practically a tenet of today's psychology and neuroscience.

I have a different take on the problem of personal identity. I say that we are our life stories. Someone's personal identity is ultimately constituted by that individual's life story. Moreover, God is tuned into every person's life story. And God sees all our life stories interweaving.

The nature of consciousness itself shows how essential narratives, or stories, are for individual personal identity. The moment a significant new event occurs in a person's life, the conscious mind acts to fold that event into the person's ongoing life story.

Hence, personal consciousness is pointed in the direction of a continuing narrative of that person's life. That is, the conscious mind focuses on keeping a narration flowing of that person's life as it unfolds.

A large part of personal consciousness comes in story form. Much of the mind is occupied with keeping track of people's stories, or narratives. That someone's conscious mind keeps track of that individual's life story is remarkable enough. But that same person's mind keeps track of lots of other individuals' life stories as well. Many of those other life stories are those of people the individual knows as relatives, friends or acquaintances. Yet numerous other life stories of historical personages, public figures or even fictional characters are also held within that same, single individual's conscious mind.

Story consciousness makes up a large portion of ordinary consciousness. The physical world may be made of atoms. But the human world is made of stories. And God watches and keeps track of and participates in all the life stories that ever were or will be. Indeed, as Ellie Wiesel said, God made people because God loves stories. So I think that we are God's stories.

I think some people realize this for themselves as they grow old. I once worked for about a year as a geriatric psychiatrist serving elderly patients in a university town. Some of my patients suffered from dementia due to Alzheimer's disease, Pick's disease or other conditions. However, the majority of the patients who came to the clinic were cognitively sharp. They were generally accomplished, distinguished members of the local community. They came to see me primarily for situational stress, or sometimes because of loneliness, or to have someone to talk to, as I soon realized.

As elderly people tend to do, my patients often looked back and reflected on the lives they led and reminisced. Repeatedly during that year I heard the same poignant remark from distinguished elderly men and women. For they commented that the older they became, the stronger an uncanny impression developed that their life had been a script, or story, or play, or movie. They used various terms to describe the impression.

That idea may seem unusual when you first hear it. However, it is actually a normal developmental phase of aging. My patients' observations in no way resembled psychotic thinking or delusions. They sensed that their lives had somehow been a script. That some aging people report this is a common and normal experience.

At first, I wondered whether what my patients were telling me might be a local tradition, or folklore. Perhaps it was a folk belief in that area that aging people begin to view their lives in retrospect as a script. Then, years later, I heard renowned mythologist Joseph Campbell say that same thing about his experience of aging. Subsequently, I have heard this same comment from elderly people in various parts of the United States, Canada and Europe. So I assume that this is a fairly common experience of reflective elderly people. I also suspect that many people reading this will be able to confirm this observation for themselves. Just ask around among bright, articulate elderly people whom you know personally. Hearing someone whom you know describe this experience makes it particularly fascinating.

In the meantime, a careful logical thinker would have reason, at this point, to accuse me of committing a fallacy. In fact, it would be one of the logical fallacies that Aristotle identified in his pioneering work on patterns of fallacious reasoning. Specifically, an objector might argue that I have taken one limited aspect of culture - the theater - and used it to characterize all human reality. That would be a fallacious use of a metaphor - a figurative expression - by treating it as a literal meaning. I would be saying (metaphorically) that life is a play while acting as though I were talking literally.

I understand the objection, but I think that things happened the other way around. The idea that life is a story did not arise from metaphorically extending the idea of the theater. Rather, I think that the theater arose from the idea that aging people develop that their lives have been scripts or stories.

In ancient Athens, a chorus performed yearly during a traditional harvest festival. The chorus sang stories of old Greek heroes. During one performance, for reasons unknown, a performer stepped forward from the chorus and spoke his own lines. When Thespis violated and entrenched tradition it created a sensation. The crowd went wild and demanded more of this new exciting form of entertainment.

Competitiveness is among the more conspicuous traits of the ancient Greeks' mentality. The Olympic Games prove my point. Hence, when the new entertainment stirred the crowd, the king decreed a contest. A race was on to see who could write the best play to perform in the newborn theater.

The big winners, over several decades, were Aeschylus, then Sophocles, then Euripides. The three gained immortal fame and their plays are still performed and studied today. Fifty years after its inception, the theater had gained the status of a profession. Originally, theaters were temples of gods and goddesses.

Why did that development take place so rapidly? What gave the theater its instant and inherent appeal? Aeschylus, Sophocles, and Euripides - three wise men - thought about and reflected on human life. Their wisdom still shines through their plays many centuries later.

They probably realized that old people look back on their lives as scripted stories. That is something that observant, reflective people realize for themselves. The Greek dramatists could have observed that as easily as we observe it today. Flattening the ground in an area created a place out in the open to act out life stories for people to see.

That is a spontaneous, smooth, natural process of development. The process is grounded in the insight that elderly people view their lives in retrospect as scripted stories. Each individual is conscious of a personal life story as it unfolds. Why do narratives occupy such a large portion of the conscious mind? Is the narrative dimension of consciousness necessary for understanding God or communicating with God? Do we need stories to learn about God? Do we need narrative consciousness to have relationships with God?

I don't think that stories and narrative consciousness are the only means of understanding God, or communicating with God or having relationships with God. Certainly there are additional means of doing so. People also encounter God in near-death experiences or in mystical visions, for example.

Even so, many religious people, perhaps the majority of them, depend mostly on stories for thinking about God and relating to God. For instance, millions of worshippers base their faith primarily on the Bible. And to a significant extent the Bible is made up of stories or narratives.

So I say that we are God's stories. We have a

narrative connection with God, along with some other kinds of connections. And when we die we review our entire life story in the loving presence of God. In God, we see connections between our life stories and the life stories of other people we knew while we were alive.

A few years ago, I lectured on near-death experiences at a Hindu ashram. During my lecture, I discussed my ideas about personal identity, life reviews and a life as a story. After my lecture, the Swami of the ashram spoke up and told me that Hindus had reached the same conclusion. Life is a drama or play and the world is a kind of theater - or a spiritual theater.

I can step back and view my own life as a story or play. But it is hard to maintain that perspective for a long period of time. After all, life is an intrinsically immersive experience. I am a self-conscious subject of experience who is immersed in my own life story. I can grasp that fact by mentally distancing myself and taking a narrative stance on my own life. Then, I can sustain that perspective in a kind of philosophical reverie or trance-like state of consciousness. Soon, though, some personal annoyance intrudes and instantly I am immersed again in the details - sometimes the irritating details - of my life story.

Life comes at us relentlessly, and often bursts in unbidden on our most insightful philosophical reflections. Nevertheless, what we glimpse briefly but repeatedly in our "Aha!" moments can eventually settle lastingly in our minds. A bi-level state of awareness is attainable in which someone can view their life as God's story while experientially immersed in that life.

An idea can be "good to think with", as Greek philosophers liked to say. They would entertain an idea just because thinking about it might engender new and interesting insights or discoveries. The idea of a life as a story is good to think with when we investigate the question of life after death.

The great philosopher and historian David Hume said that reincarnation is the only view of the afterlife that a philosophically-minded person could contemplate. Maybe Hume thought so because as an historian he knew that narratives, or stories, are essential for understanding human nature. Reincarnation is perhaps the most story-centered conception of life after death.

Supposedly, when we finish one life story we die and go through some incomprehensible process in another dimension. We then emerge from that other dimension and begin a new life story centered in a new body and usually in a different locale. When that new life story ends in death of the body we repeat the incomprehensible process culminating in another rebirth. Authoritative sources disagree among themselves concerning how many such cycles an individual must complete and why. They also disagree concerning what the individual's fate will be upon completing the final life story.

Earlier, we discussed people who like to think and argue about whether or not God "exists." One topic they frequently argue about is what is known as the problem of evil. Presumably, God is loving, God knows everything and God can do anything. Why then, some ask, do terrible things happen? This argument is often raised to suggest that God does not "exist." Reincarnation, together with the story perspective on life, can put a different spin on the problem of evil.

I presented the following scenario to numerous audiences totaling hundreds of people. Suppose you contracted an infectious illness that required you to live alone on an island for ten years. You are flown to the island in a cargo plane carrying a supply of food, water and medicine to last a decade. Happily, there is enough additional cargo space for a DVD player and, let's say, 5000 movies on DVD's. Given that scenario, would you choose all comedies?

Virtually everyone I asked that question answered "No!" Then, I asked them, "Would you also choose some tragedies?" And everyone I asked that question answered, "Yes!" Then, I asked them, "When you were alone on the island watching a tragedy, would you be crying?" And again everyone I asked that question answered, "Yes, I would be." For after all, crying is the emotional response we expect to experience when we are watching a tragedy.

We choose to watch a tragedy understanding full well that we will be upset, distressed, sad, and crying while we watch it. We also understand beforehand that watching a tragedy will be a self-contained, time-limited experience. The experience will be over before too long and we will get through the experience alive. We might even anticipate experiencing what Aristotle called catharsis, a discharge or release of pent-up negative emotions.

Imagine yourself in another dimension, the afterlife realm, preparing for your next incarnation into this world. Imagine all sorts of life stories spread out before you and you have some degree of input into what your next life will be like. And you know that whatever life story you enter will be a time-limited, temporary experience. You will live that life, die, and return to the afterlife realm. You know that most if not all life stories involve some degree of strife, heartbreak, distress, sadness, tragedy and suffering. You understand that entering a life story, you become immersed in it and forget that it is one of God's stories.

That is the picture Plato and others painted of a higher dimension of life from which our consciousness emerges at birth into this world. Of course, in reality the words prompt us to try and imagine the unimaginable. That higher dimension defies the mind's inbuilt system of time-space coordinates. Nevertheless, the picture accords well with the sense reflective elders develop that life is somehow a scripted story.

Plato said that event boundaries ordinarily keep that higher dimension separate from this life. You experienced event boundaries many times. Suppose you are in your living room and you decide to fetch something from the kitchen. Then as soon as you walk through the kitchen door you forget what you went in there to do. Similarly, when we emerge into this world we forget the prelude to our life story that occurred in another state of consciousness.

Projecting myself mentally into that prior state, I can easily imagine choosing a life story full of hardships and difficulties. That is not to say that I would delight in those hardships when living amidst them. No, I would be protesting, agonizing, sobbing, wishing they would go away. That is what I signed up for to begin with, then forgot about it. In that prior state, I had an educational plan or even an interesting experience in mind. People stand in line for a long time to get onto a roller coaster. Yet they know full well that when they are zooming along upside down at ninety miles an hour they won't want to be there.

I can imagine choosing to experience many different life stories full of all sorts of miseries, perplexities and challenges, for educational purposes. Even if that higher dimension allowed me to choose only a single life story, I cannot say I would necessarily choose a comedy. I might want to choose the most interesting or instructive life story. For I would understand in advance that the story is time-limited and will end in my returning to my place of origin. The view of life as a story harmonizes neatly with the concept of reincarnation but with other possibilities as well.

Billions of people live in cultures that officially subscribe to the concept of reincarnation, whatever particular individuals in those cultures might think. Lots of other people live in cultures that officially subscribe to a different concept in which life is a one-shot deal. In that concept, the afterlife is a cosmic justice system of rewards and punishments in Heaven and Hell. I think that in reality that system is meaningless and incoherent. God is not interested in justice. God sees a much bigger picture than constricted human ideas of justice and injustice and retribution and revenge.

# CHAPTER FIVE

# God and Justice

In about 1968 a touring company of a Broadway musical comedy performed one night in Charlottesville, Virginia. I was a graduate student in philosophy at the University of Virginia at the time and my wife and I attended the show. We sat in front row seats.

I don't remember which musical comedy it was, but I do vividly remember the sublime comic villain in the play. He wore a sinister black cape and a black stovepipe hat. His voice dripped with malice as he treated the other characters in the play with calculated meanness.

When the show came to an end the curtain went

down and the audience burst into enthusiastic applause. After a while, the cast came out for curtain calls. First, the hero and heroine dashed onto the stage to loud cheers and a mounting wave of applause. Then the supporting actors and actresses swept in a happy throng to the front of the stage. When they did a chorus of cheers grew louder and louder.

Then, at last, the villain himself stepped forth into the spotlight and he took center stage. And when he did the audience instantly fell totally silent. From our seats right in front of the stage it felt as though the silence lasted for an eternity. In reality, it was probably at most a couple of seconds, but time seemed to stretch out or stand still.

Then, suddenly, from behind me I heard a collective gasp. A lot of people in the audience, at the same moment, audibly drew in a breath in shock and surprise. They emerged from a trance-like immersion in the play back to mundane reality. They were realizing that the man standing in the spotlight was an actor who had entertained them by performing the role of a villain in the play.

Behind me, I heard scattered pockets of people in the audience burst into applause. Then people all through the audience started clapping. The applause grew louder and louder and then people in the audience were cheering. In the end, the villain got the loudest, longest cheers and applause of all.

While immersed in the show, people perceived the actor's words and actions as evil. When the show ended, their minds momentarily got confused in the transition back to everyday life. Then, fully out of the trance, they applauded the actor for a fine performance. What appeared as evil in one framework reappeared as something positive in a more inclusive reality.

Similar mental and spiritual shifts occur during near-death experiences. Something that severe religions condemn as an "abomination" or claim is "forbidden by God" may evaporate into insignificance on the other side. My dear friend and mentor George Ritchie gave an illuminating example.

George had been raised in a strict Presbyterian religion when he was pronounced dead of double lobar pneumonia when he was 20 years old. He was revived and his near-death experience dramatically changed his life. He got out of his body and experienced a detailed panoramic review of his life in the presence of Christ.

George said that by that time in his life he had an active sexual career, not all of it with the opposite sex. Yet according to strict Presbyterian ideology sexual departures were the worst sins, and would surely send you straight to Hell. So there George was with all those supposed sins displayed visibly around him in a panorama and in the presence of Christ's complete overwhelming love.

A beautiful smile of relief and joy appeared on George's face as he remembered Christ's reaction to the supposed sins. The surprise still registered in George's voice as he told me about this decades after the experience. George said, "He didn't even mention them!"

Justice is a set of rules and principles people developed to regulate their lives in this world. People take familiar aspects of this life to construct their mental pictures of the next life. Many people picture the afterlife as a justice system for dispensing rewards and punishments in Heaven and Hell. Then, they try to pass off their mental construction as God's idea.

God is not interested in justice. God has a much better idea. God loves and educates, rather than dispensing justice. So why would I even bring up Hell in a book about God's love?

The idea of Hell scares many people away from God and keeps them from enjoying happy personal relationships with God. The idea of Hell is a citadel of self-righteousness. The Christian Church originally conceptualized Hell as entertainment. Watching the damned being tormented in Hell below was among the delights the Church promised would await the saved in Heaven above. Early Christian works of art illustrated the theme.

Nothing much has changed. Today's religious believers who threaten us with Hell have that same attitude. To be honest, how could anyone not notice their self-satisfied smirk?

Don't run away from a relationship with God because of associating God with Hell. God has no part in Hell. Hell has to do with the vagaries of human personality.

A certain kind of religious person becomes preoccupied by thoughts and images of Hell, Satan and demonic deception. These believers experience a curious inner delight when they imagine people they dislike burning in Hell. They get a kick out of telling other people that they are going to Hell. Usually, the supposed reason is that the people don't believe in or accept some specific point of religious doctrine. The religious believers might mentally consign a person to Hell for not believing in the Trinity, for instance. Or they may mentally consign someone to Hell for not agreeing that the Bible says such-and-such. Here we have another manifestation of Bible abuse.

Satan, demons and Hell occupy the foreground of these religious believers' minds. God sort of goes out of focus and recedes into the background. These believers trot God out mainly as an enforcer. God is a legalistic, somewhat vindictive character who is ready to pounce on anyone who doesn't swear by the correct set of Bible beliefs. The religious believers I am talking about are always looking for an opening to get back to their favorite subject of Satan, demons, and Hell. God is an afterthought.

I try my best to call anything I talk about by its right name. What should we call religious believers who focus enthusiastically on Hell, demons and Satan? Those believers often call themselves fundamentalists. They apparently think that "fundamentalism" harks back to old, old times and the original Christian beliefs. But that is inaccurate. Milton and Lyman Stewart were conservative Protestant brothers from California who got rich in their oil business. In 1910 they commissioned a series of religious tracts entitled *The Fundamentals*. A conservative Baptist editor tacked the "-ists" on in 1920. Subsequently, the word got bent out of shape and took on negative, pejorative connotations. "Fundamentalism" has been applied to such a wide and divergent range of people, doctrines and movements that it is too vague for our purposes.

Dwelling on devils, Satanic deceptions, invisible demons trying to corrupt Biblical teachings and people burning in Hell has its own rightful name. The right name for that manner of speaking and thinking is demonology. Look the word up in the standard dictionary and see for yourself. Demonology is the belief that demons really exist and in league with Satan deceive, torment and afflict human beings and deliver them to Hell. If a person actually believes that then by definition that person is a demonologist.

Demonologists are prone to nonsensical thinking. The infractions that demonologists condemn take place within the brief few decades of a person's life. Yet because of those brief supposed transgressions that person must suffer eons upon endless eons of horrendous punishment in Hell.

The idea of justice includes the notion of a balance between an offense and its punishment. Justice is personified as a woman wearing a blindfold and holding a balance, or scale. The concept is that the punishment must fit the crime. Accordingly, calling everlasting horrendous punishment for a brief, fleeting offense "justice" is meaningless, unintelligible nonsense.

My daughter once took me aback when she said, "Daddy, I want to go to Hell." Knowing Carol as I do, I realized that there was probably something pretty deep on her mind. So I asked her to explain.

She told me that there were lots of self-righteous religious kids at school. The religious kids were constantly preaching to the other kids. The young religious fanatics were trying to convert laid-back students with scare stories about Hell. So Carol said she would rather be in Hell with her kind-hearted friends than in Heaven with the know-it-alls.

I told her that Mark Twain made that same

observation. He said, "Heaven for the climate, but Hell for the company."

Carol laughed and said, "Yeah! That's what I mean."

God is not interested in justice. Justice is an aspect of life in this world. And the idea of Hell is a nonsensical distortion of the notion of justice that bears no relationship to God.

Still, there is a common phenomenon of human life that some still faintly associate with the idea of God punishing them. I am referring to the seemingly magical way in which people somehow get their just desserts in life. Or, as you often hear it said, "What goes around comes around." This is a strange enough and common enough occurrence that it deserves serious consideration.

I once treated someone badly for quite a long time. I felt I had been disrespected and disgraced and wronged and was justified in taking revenge. Years passed and then as if by magic I found myself in the directly opposite situation, on the receiving end. I was being demeaned and berated and reviled by somebody for no good reason at all. However, my tormentor was ten times more skilled at cruel, harsh, meanness than I had been.

Some say that the unconscious somehow brings such reversals about from a guilty conscience. Some others might allude to karma. Yet others feel that God must be punishing them, dispensing retributive justice. I definitely felt God's touch in my own situation but I don't think God had justice in mind. God's purpose was education, not justice. Truthfully, the only way we can understand the hurt we inflict on others is by directly experiencing that hurt ourselves. And I realized that it really helps when the hurt is amplified to bring it to our attention and reinforce the lesson.

So the entire time of my ordeal I was cheering God on. I was thinking, thank you, thank you, thank you, thank you, oh, thank you, dear God. That kind of experience does not have anything to do with justice. God is an expert at the best conceivable kind of education there can be.

Hell is not the only religious doctrine that makes people afraid of getting close to God in a personal way. Incredibly, some people cannot even think of God except in the context of a specific religion, or religion in general. But God is greater than any one religion and greater even than all the religions rolled into one.

Religion is a mixed bag, though. The many elements of religion have to be considered on a case-by-case basis. Loving God doesn't require us to be religious. God doesn't care whether or not we join a religion.

# CHAPTER SIX

# God and Religion

An elderly Episcopalian priest once startled me when he said, "I want religion without God." And I surprised myself when, without thinking, I said back to him, "I want God without religion."

I assume the priest was thinking of rituals and ceremonies. He cherished the aesthetics of religious behaviors. The performance aspect of church services felt good to him.

To be honest, though, I am not a social creature. Rituals and ceremonies don't have any meaningful impact on me. To me, rituals are boring, tedious and a waste of time I could spend learning something, or watching the news. The way it looks to me, rituals are just another excuse people have to socialize or show off their new clothes to friends and acquaintances. For a solitary, shrinking violet like me, rituals and ceremonies don't have anything to do with God. And for me, God is where the action is.

Religion does not have a monopoly on God. God doesn't care whether or not we join a religion. Plenty of people are walking around out there who have strong relationships with God, and who love God, and who want no part of religion. I am one of them myself.

A fine, deep, devoted relationship with God can be completely in line with an inward life apart from religious activities, beliefs, or organizations. You don't need a religion to love God or for God to love you. People who seem unable to separate God from their religion, or from religion in general, are making a big mistake, it seems to me. And a mistake like that can interfere with someone's relationship with God.

The Episcopalian priest I mentioned earlier is a case in point. He got so engrossed in rituals and ceremonies and fancy outfits that he lost track of his relationship with God. The trappings gratified him so much that he pushed God out of the picture.

For the same reason, incredibly, an atheists' association actually formed a church! They said they had many fond childhood memories of participating in church services. They said that although they think that there is no God, they still find comfort and enjoyment in the social and ceremonial aspects of religion.

In their books, some writers take an entirely negative stance on religion. They like to recite horror after unutterable horror that people perpetrated on their fellow human beings in the name of religion. Writers of that type don't bother to balance what they write by mentioning the many good things people have done for others in the name of religion.

Please understand that this book is not a blanket condemnation of religion. Religion is a monumentally important historical, socio-cultural, psychological, spiritual aspect of human life. The study of religion encompasses a whole host of fascinating people, practices, doctrines, movements and institutions. Scholars of religion study pilgrimages, monasticism, martyrdom, sacred mountains, tree worship, holy books and extraordinary states of consciousness like conversion and mystical experiences. Who couldn't find something delightful, entertaining and inspiring in a list like that? Religion as an intrinsic aspect of the enthralling, curious, endlessly fascinating creatures - human beings.

What I am trying to get across is not that religion in itself is something bad. What I mean to say is that religion is not necessary to carry on a meaningful relationship with God. And my observations suggest to me that many religious people do enjoy great relationships with God. My observations also suggest to me that many people enjoy fine relationships with God without the trappings of religion. Religion is something apart and separate from God, though there are points of contact and areas of overlap. In sum, people can carry on good, engaged, vital relationships with God, regardless of whether they contextualize their relationship in terms of religion. And God doesn't care whether we are religious or not.

Personally, I am very cautious in my judgements and statements about religion. I am not religious myself and I don't belong to any church or other religious organization. Nonetheless, I study religion for its inherent interest and its relevance to history, sociology, psychology and philosophy. I am also cautious in my judgements and statements because three times in my life I scoffed at religious practices, but later corrected myself. For later I realized that those practices stemmed from valuable spiritual experiences.

Specifically, I used to think people were vain, conceited or unreflective for kneeling in church, shouting "Praise God!" or saying prayers of thanks before meals. I thought such people were trying to flatter God, or get on God's good side, by meaningless rituals. How ridiculous, I thought. How can they possibly think that God, the Supreme Being, wants people to bow and scrape and grovel? I assumed they were trying to get their wishes granted by pumping up

God's ego.

I admit I was contemptuous of such pointless religious practices. I thought that these practices misconstrued God as a narrow, pompous, thin-skinned, ego-obsessed being, susceptible to manipulation by human beings. To me, it seemed incredible that people thought they could get ahead in life by stroking God's ego!

Now, some people do seem to have that astonishing egoistic attitude toward Almighty God. At the same time, I acknowledge that kneeling before God, praising God and thanking God before meals sometimes makes sense in themselves, apart from religious rituals. Sometimes those acts are spontaneous expressions of profound spiritual emotions or transcendent experiences.

During a dark time of my life, in July 1991, I was in deep despair and I wanted to die. Suddenly, the presence of God descended on me unbidden, and I felt a deep compassion that was palpable and yet completely beyond the reach of words. I had been sitting upright in a chair, but when I felt the presence of God I crumpled into a relaxed heap and melted blissfully to the floor. God was not interested in a show of respect from me. And I did not kneel down with the intention of appeasing God or showing respect to God. I slumped down because, as I learned, you can't stand up in the presence of God. God's presence is pleasurably overwhelming in an awesome, transporting, unforgettable, unmistakable life-altering way. George Ritchie described God's irresistible sway over consciousness as "like you're being fiercely hypnotized." God's presence casts such a powerful spell that your muscles relax and you can't stand up so you collapse to the ground. Yet it is a completely comforting and relaxed and awed state that you would gladly continue to experience on and on into eternity.

Years later, I learned the spiritual meaning of "Praise God!" For, frankly, that phrase often sounds stilted or pretentious, artificial or conventionalized. When preachers say it from behind a pulpit, or congregations shout it when the preacher prompts them, it can sound hollow or rehearsed or staged. Then, one day, all that changed for me.

Unexpectedly, I received some great news and I was overjoyed. I can't remember any thought passing through my mind. Yet suddenly I shouted "Praise God!" The words were a joyful, involuntary outburst expressing gratitude I felt, and I projected it toward God. I saw that exclaiming "Praise God!" can reach out in a spontaneous gesture that instantly connects with God.

Why did I exclaim "Praise God!"? Certainly not to try and flatter God or pander to God or get on God's good side. However, I realize that it did reflect on my mind's turning to God to get God's attention, almost as a gesture of companionship. I was expressing joyous gratitude, though not necessarily gratitude to God. Rather, it felt as though I wanted and needed to express gratitude, but not to anyone in particular. "Praise God!" was a way of drawing God's attention to a joyous experience I was having. I think "God likes to be included," as a good friend once said to me.

I don't even remember what the good news I received that day was. Instead, I remember the insight I had into the spiritual meaning of "Praise God!" "Praise God!" was my spontaneous reaching out to touch God and get God's attention.

To keep your mind tuned in to God whatever else may be happening is a hard thing to do. But the better I get at it the happier I become. And "Praise God!" can be an effective expression for making contact with God spontaneously and sharing a thrilling or happy experience with God.

Similarly, I learned that thanking God before meals is a gesture of companionship that helps keep the mind tuned in to God. A prayer of thanks like that is another way of including God in life. Besides, as you learn after a while, it makes the food taste better.

That is one reason I am so cautious about making summary judgements about religion. I grumbled about the vanity of people kneeling before God or praising God or praying to God before meals. Then, I saw each of those gestures from a different angle and in a new light. Each separate phenomenon of religious life deserves its own serious investigation and analysis. To make a general statement like "Religion is a noxious influence on humanity" is practically meaningless. We need to be specific in our criticisms and really think them through. That still leaves a lot of religious behavior that is pretty outrageous, in my opinion. One item in particular that raises my blood pressure is the audacity of those who presume to act as agents of God in political disputes.

Some Bible believers act as though they think they are directly helping out in enacting God's plan, or even acting on God's behalf. To me, the idea that God acting alone cannot get a thing done, but needs human assistance, is pretty perplexing. The notion of God's helpers reminds me of Santa Claus, not God.

Are they saying that God has areas of weakness, inability or incapacity that they can remedy? Are God's human helpers needed because God alone is unable to make certain events take place? Plus, how do the helpers know exactly what God wants to happen in complicated social situations? After all, Bible-believing helpers usually try to intervene in complex social issues that are hot topics of contentious public and political debate. They pretend they are adding God's two cents' worth to debates about prayer in schools, gay marriage and the theory of evolution. In past ages, they pretended to add God's two cents' worth to lots of other scientific, moral, political or cultural controversies. They once told us that God required us to believe that the sun revolves around the Earth, for instance. Periodically, they still pretend to tell us how God wants us to cut our hair, or wants us to dress. They pretend to know that God doesn't want us to listen to certain kinds of music and will send us to Hell if we do.

The trouble is, they don't know they are pretending. Their entire attitude toward God and the Bible and their religion is pretense - pretending to know things they don't know. Personally, I cannot imagine any other outcome of constant pretense like that other than profound inner turmoil and dissatisfaction. This is another manifestation of Bible abuse.

All this points to the futile absurdity of the idea of people chipping in to get God's grand design accomplished on Earth. To me, a pushy certitude about what God's will is in complicated social controversies smacks of stubborn ignorance. And their personal eagerness to intervene in the name of God and the Bible seems awfully presumptuous. In my experience, humble prayerful submission to God's superior knowledge and perspective is a wiser policy.

I once was wrestling with a vexatious problem and it was getting to me. At long last, I just threw up my hands and turned the problem over to God in prayer. Shortly afterwards, the problem resolved itself and quickly went away. A few days later, I mentioned the incident to my friend and mentor George Ritchie. George smiled his characteristic impish smile and he said, "Surrender is the most powerful prayer."

Incidentally, religion is not the sole source of

glitches in our thinking about God. Mix-ups occur even when you are in a satisfying ongoing relationship with God, free of religious preoccupations. For instance, I often find myself trying not to impose on God!

Some minor but irritating difficulty arises in my life and my first impulse is to pray to God for relief. Then, I think better of it. I think, no, I don't want to bother God with such a trivial thing. After all, God must be busy, and I don't want to impose on God.

At first blush, that may sound like a polite gesture. Then, when you think it through, a different picture emerges. My thinking that I, Raymond Moody, limited person that I am, can impose on God is nothing short of egomaniacal. Even if we were to rid ourselves entirely of religion, ego would still be around to do its dirty work.

Personally, I am opposed to the cult of self-esteem. Many psychologists teach that it is important for people to maintain positive self-esteem. My life experience has taught me the opposite lesson, though. I try to keep my self-esteem as low as possible. For the greater danger in life is ego.

I have a simple formula: Ego equals pain. If you think about it, you will see that whenever your ego is involved, it is always a painful situation. I have managed to shrink my ego to a less troublesome size. Of course, that statement itself sounds pretty egotistical. And it would be if I had gone to the mountaintop, burned the incense, laid on the bed of nails, and so on. In reality, though, I whittled my ego down by damn near killing myself with it.

My own ego trip was jealousy. Once you escape from an ego trip, however, and look back on it, it seems dreamlike. When you are in it, it seems so completely real. Yet in retrospect you say, "How could I possibly have been thinking like that?" All ego trips have that same dreamlike structure. For that reason, one ego trip is enough.

My point here is that religion is not the only means

we have of running away from an open and honest relationship with God. Our own egos can serve that purpose, too. That doesn't get religion off the hook, though. And there is still plenty of blame to go around.

Religion has also exerted a baneful influence on another intrinsic human value - the quest for knowledge. Religious authorities have repeatedly, deliberately, sometimes violently suppressed the pursuit of truth. And that brings us to the next of my thoughts about God. God is no excuse for ignorance.

# CHAPTER SEVEN

# God and Knowledge

"Five minutes without oxygen causes irreparable damage to the brain." That statement has practically become a tenet of common sense. Certainly it is a useful clinical rule of thumb to keep in mind when you are trying to revive someone from a cardiac arrest. Yet there are exceptions. Some of them make sense and a few of them are unfathomable mysteries.

Sometimes, young people rescued after being immersed under cold water for long periods survive with no brain damage. What is known as the diving reflex is at work in cases like these. Dousing the face with cold water shunts blood to the brain in preference to less vital organs. Certain extraordinary medical procedures also keep the brain viable for long periods without oxygen.

Even so, I know of some cases of survival following long-duration cardiac arrests that are frankly inexplicable. Often, the doctors involved interpret these extraordinary cases as miracles, or as spiritual experiences. For instance, Dr. George Ritchie had no heartbeat and no signs of life for more than nine minutes. A ward attendant discovered George already apparently dead in a hospital bed. The medical staff had no way of determining how long he had been in that state when he was found apparently dead. And nine minutes elapsed before the ward physician revived George with an adrenaline injection directly into the heart. The physician stated many years later that George's case remained the most remarkable situation he had encountered in decades of medical practice.

I knew a woman whose doctor told me that her cardiac arrest lasted for forty minutes. Unique, intensely personal considerations, not medical factors, prompted him to try and revive her. Her profound near-death experience touched everyone who knew her and transformed her doctor.

I have known more than twenty people with near-death experiences whose cardiac arrests lasted for longer than is consistent with current medical knowledge. They were all interesting, engaging people and only a few had minor neurological symptoms left over from their medical crises. For the most part, their near-death experiences went beyond the more typical cases. In those rare cases, people glimpsed transcendent realms, higher dimensions of reality extending beyond the framework of more familiar near-death experiences. They got out of their bodies, sped through a tunnel into a bright light, met deceased relatives and friends and reviewed their lives. But then, unlike many other people, these individuals' consciousness deepened and they became aware of higher levels or states far beyond physical existence.

One of these higher realms - my personal favorite - is what might be roughly compared to a super-university, or think tank. George Ritchie saw this place. He said that if you mentally squeezed CalTech, MIT, Harvard, Yale and Princeton into one, you still couldn't imagine it. Other people who glimpsed this transcendent realm of knowledge expressed similar frustrations at their inability to describe what they saw.

The beings in the realm of knowledge were busily pursuing their research and were focused on trying to find out the truth. George was a brilliant man who graduated from college when he was twenty years old and was exceptionally knowledgeable concerning scientific subjects. Yet as he viewed these beings he had no idea what they were studying. George saw into one area or aspect of this realm that was comparable to a library or repository of knowledge. George said that he saw one section of the library that stored the holy books of the universe!

One woman who saw the realm of knowledge had no intellectual interests prior to her near-death experience. Her relatives told me that up to that point her reading material was strictly limited to romance novels. Yet after her experience she became an avid reader of books on psychology and religious studies. I discussed many of these texts with her and she showed in-depth understanding and comprehension of them.

One detail of what George said about the realm of knowledge troubles me, I must admit. During George's near-death experience, Christ guided him through a sort of tour of transcendent realms. Christ showed George the realm of knowledge and the two of them gazed together at beings who were single-mindedly seeking knowledge. George said that Christ was obviously very proud of these determined seekers. "But," George continued, "they couldn't see Him."

George's remark reminded me of something Nietzsche said: "The opposite of love is not hate but the dispassionate pursuit of truth." So am I off beam in my lifelong passion for learning and seeking new knowledge? George certainly didn't seem concerned about my fate, so I don't worry - at least not much.

For I am a learning addict and I just can't help it. I

love learning new things and curiosity has driven my life as a philosophy professor, writer and psychiatrist. History, science, medicine, psychology, sociology, literary studies and other fields of knowledge fascinate me. And I think that in the long run, acquiring new knowledge is the most fun anyone can have while living this life.

That is another aspect of my personality that occasionally brings me into conflict with organized religion. I had an experience in high school that still troubles me to this day. I was reading an insightful book on the mind and I recommended it to one of my classmates. To my astonishment, he replied that he was not allowed to read that book. "What? Why?" I asked in amazement and incomprehension.

My friend explained that his religion kept a list of books that members were expressly forbidden to read. I don't remember what his religion was and don't even remember whether I knew it at that time. Either way, the authoritarian thinking behind that list struck me as utterly abhorrent, or even disgusting. Apparently, the authorities in his religion made a concerted effort to keep their membership ignorant of established knowledge. I assume that the authorities wanted to prevent new knowledge from disturbing their rigid religious ideology.

God is no excuse for ignorance. In fact, many people with near-death experiences reported that God encouraged them to learn during their life reviews. Of course, the main focus of life reviews is on the individual's capacity to love oneself and others. Even so, many reported that God would also focus in on times in which they had been learning something. Many reported that God indicated that the process of learning will continue after death. Many told me that they gathered from their life reviews that they will continue acquiring new knowledge quite literally for eternity.

Many people took this lesson to heart. After recovering their health, they hurried to nearby colleges or universities to sign up for courses. Some even entered long-term educational programs preparing themselves for new professions. I have heard this for decades from numerous individuals. Hence, I assume that extending one's education is a fairly common after-effect of near-death experiences.

Still, some religions do try to keep their members in the dark about important historical, psychological, medical or scientific knowledge. But this is a human foible that doesn't have anything to do with God. Incredibly, many people are scared to say "I don't know." Perhaps overly stern teachers frightened and humiliated them when they were children. Perhaps someone berated them when they were unable to answer a question. And sadly, some severe religions encourage this attitude.

Some proponents of ideological religions seem to think they already know everything and they quote the Bible to back up their opinion. This is another common form of Bible abuse. Perhaps on some level they are afraid that their religious beliefs might evaporate into thin air, if pressed too hard. Whatever their motivation, religious ideologues don't experience the joy of new knowledge. They deprive themselves and their families of the fun of pushing back the frontiers of what is known. And, incredibly, they do this in the name of God!

God isn't about fear and God doesn't condone willful ignorance. That is what I hear from people who met God during near-death experiences. Censorship and condemning new ideas is a function of narrow-minded people. God doesn't have anything to do with it.

Severely religious people still try to hold back the progress of knowledge. Theories about the creation of the world are one of the main arenas in which they try to exercise censorship. But I say that God's creativity is vastly greater than they imagine. In reality, God continually creates everything.

## CHAPTER EIGHT

# God and Creation

The flow of creativity is one of the most exhilarating, joyous experiences of life. Creativity is an extraordinary state of consciousness and a mysterious power of the mind. Thinking up new concepts and stories feels to me much like a mystical experience. Ancient Greeks thought of creativity as an experiential encounter with spiritual beings - the muses. That is still how creativity feels to many artists, writers, thinkers and inventors in today's world. Numerous artists told me that their creative work seems to come from a source outside or above them, not from within them.

I feel God meets us halfway in creativity. When immersed in writing a new book, I frequently consult with God. I pray, asking for the right word, or advice or guidance. I ask God to lead me to help my readers or inspire, comfort or instruct them with a good message. And I sometimes feel inspiration coming from God. Creativity is definitely part of my personal relationship with God. I feel that my creativity and God's creativity work together. I enjoy my relationship with God and creativity is one way of interacting directly with God.

The mystery of the creation of the universe is an ancient, deep philosophical problem. To comprehend the creation of the world may well be beyond the powers of the mind. On one side, is an assumed previous void-like state of nonexistent nothingness. On the other side is the present state of the entire, incomprehensible immense universe and its physical reality. And a vast chasm of unimaginability and incomprehension separates those two states. The mind is incapable of thinking in a smooth, unbroken line from the assumed previous void-like state of nothingness to the present state of existence. The mind boggles when it tries to bridge the chasm separating them. The mind struggles to fill in the gap.

Now, to me, this is an exciting, delightful state of affairs. I love wrestling with perplexing philosophical problems that defy the rational mind. To me, it is irresistible to keep on delving into the problem, trying to come up with an original approach or innovative solution. I am highly tolerant of ambiguity.

Not so for some others, however. People with rigid or authoritarian personalities have trouble with ambiguity. They want to plug the gap right now. Not having a definite answer drives them crazy.

In Genesis, the Bible says that God created the world in six days and then rested on the seventh day. Genesis tells how God created Adam and Eve, the first man and first woman, and planted them in the Garden of Eden. Most people in our society are aware of this story, at least in outline.

A few years ago, Biblical creationists filed a suit in Federal court. They wanted to require the Biblical story of creation to be taught alongside the theory of evolution in public school biology courses. They were trying to compel your children and my children to endure religious indoctrination in publicly funded science courses. Their rationale, supposedly, was that the Biblical account should be taught as an alternative hypothesis to Darwin's theory of evolution. Fortunately, the judge, himself a conservative, saw through the ruse. He rebuked the creationists for trying to sneak their religious ideology into public education.

Religious creationists argued that their program would be an effective exercise in critical thinking. Comparing and contrasting the Biblical story with the theory of evolution would help students test and evaluate contending hypotheses and explanations. I agree with them in part, though, because I am a creationist, too. But I am a New Creationist, not an old-fashioned Biblical creationist. I don't think Biblical creationists go nearly far enough in their creationism. They say that God created the world in six days about 5000 years ago. But I say that God is much more deeply involved in creation than that. I say that God is creating everything all the time. God is not a distant, abstract figure who created the world and then backed away from it. God is vitally active in an ongoing creation.

The Bible is a book that divides people as much as it unites people. That does not mean that the Bible divides people just into believers and unbelievers. The Bible divides believers themselves into multitudes of clashing sects with their own conflicting interpretations of the Bible. Rival sects of Bible believers once waged horrific wars against each other that left legions of them dead on the battlefield.

Therefore, that Biblical creationists might succeed in forcing their doctrine into the public school curriculum is not a realistic prospect. As soon as that happened, other sects of Bible believers would protest. The protesters would insist that, no, it is in their own conflicting interpretation of the Genesis story that is the true Biblical one. So their true interpretation of the creation story in Genesis is the one that ought to be taught in public schools, instead. And the fight would be on yet again.

My New Creationism can help Biblical creationists out with their main objective. They wanted to use the Genesis account of creation to help students to learn critical thinking. That is an excellent idea, and I think it should be done. As a New Creationist I know how to get that done without committing Bible abuse, which was Biblical creationists' mistake.

The mystery of the creation of the world naturally captivates people. Wondering about how the world originated seems to be an inherent propensity of the human mind. Cultures and religions all over the world came up with innumerable fascinating creation stories. Those creation stories are well worth studying for what they can tell us about our minds and cultures.

My course would be taught as a humanities course, not in a science department. In my course, the Genesis creation story would be taught alongside other creation stories of people and cultures and religions of the whole world. That is the proper procedure. The Genesis story is not a scientific theory so comparing it to a scientific theory like evolution makes no sense.

Creation stories of cultures around the globe are divided into numerous types and categories. The account in Genesis is an example of the creation from nothing type, or creation ex nihilo. Creation ex nihilo stories are especially popular in monotheistic religions. In creation ex nihilo stories, the divinity usually creates the world by thinking, speaking or breathing. In one story, God created the world by dancing.

In another type of creation story, the Creator is a sort of craftsman who creates the world from matter that already exists, rather than from nothing. Plato's dialogue *Timaeus* contains an example of this type of creation story. Such stories interpret creation on the analogy of a human skill or craft.

Yet other types of stories tell of creation from a cosmic egg or creation from the division of a primordial unity that already exists. Such stories talk of the world being created by the division of the sky from the earth, for instance. Other stories portray creation as an emergence of people from a womb-like underworld. So many different creation stories are found around the world that a sizable book could be written on classifying them into types.

Some creation stories are unique and practically unclassifiable. The following astonishing creation story is from ancient Hindu scriptures known as the *Rig Veda*. The story is a hymn entitled the Nasaiya, or "There was Not." The author seems to acknowledge wryly that creation stories must contain elements of nonsense.

> There was neither nonexistence nor existence then; there was neither the realm of space nor the sky which is beyond. What stirred? Where? In whose protection? Was there water bottomless deep? Was there neither death nor immortality then? There was no distinguishing sign of night nor of day. That One breathed, windless, by its own impulse.

> Other than that, there was nothing

beyond. Darkness was hidden by darkness in the beginning; with no distinguishing sign, all this was water. The life force that was covered with emptiness, that One arose through the power of heat.

Desire came upon that One in the beginning; that was the first seed of the mind. Poets seeking in their heart with wisdom found the bond of existence in nonexistence. Their cord was extended across. Was there below? Was there above? There were seed-placers; there were powers. There was impulse beneath; there was giving-forth above.

Who really knows? Who will here proclaim it? When was it produced? Whence is this creation? The gods came afterwards with the creation of the universe. Who knows whence it has arisen? Whence this creation has arisen--perhaps it formed itself, or perhaps it did not--the one who looks down on it, on the highest heaven, only he knows-or perhaps he does not know.

God's creative energy and ingenuity are far greater are more immediate than we can comprehend, in my opinion. God's creation is a dynamic living process rather than something that happened once in a remote, unknowable past. I sense that God is actively, lovingly creating everything that you and I see around us. I connect God's creation with God's delightful creativity firsthand. Creativity is another way of directly encountering God.

We have been talking about various excuses people use to run away from a personal relationship with God. Recently, some believers have found another way of going off the beam. They think they have figured out how to shake down God for money.

# CHAPTER NINE

# God's Cash Register

Loving God is its own reward. I love hanging out with God. I love God's wisdom, God's sublime sense of humor, God's creativity and God's soul-filling love. Relaxing with God and talking with God and including God in my daily activities is enjoyable in itself. I can't get enough of it.

St. Augustine also talked about enjoying God. He coined a memorable oxymoron to describe the experience: "insatiable satisfaction." I get in touch with God first thing in the morning, in the evening before bed and several times in between. I do it just because it is a satisfying experience in itself.

Some evangelicals think they have figured out a method of pumping God for money. Prosperity Gospel believers read the Bible, follow a prescribed set of Biblical teachings and shower lots and lots of money on their preachers and churches. Then they expect God to send that money back to them tenfold!

The Prosperity Gospel sounds like a pyramid scheme to me. Fantasizing about having a ton of money is tremendous fun. But I think Prosperity Gospel folks have let their imaginations run away with them. Worshipping God is a different kind of activity than chasing material wealth.

God isn't an automated teller machine. Scheming to multiply your cash supply looks to me like another way of avoiding an honest, conscious relationship with God. Better to join the rat race than face the potentially terrifying prospect of a direct personal encounter with God. The Prosperity Gospel preachers encourage people to immerse themselves in the bustling economic life of America. I suspect that they do that partly to escape the complexities of spiritual life and communing with God.

I like to watch Prosperity Gospel preachers and their congregations on their television programs. If you haven't tuned in you are missing a great show. The preachers insist that God wants them and their flocks to be just as prosperous as nonbelievers seem to be. Their television shows give the impression that Prosperity Gospel folks like big houses, fancy cars, and flashy display goods.

Jim and Tammy Bakker became famous for their Praise the Lord television show and religious amusement park. They built a materialists' paradise for themselves with the proceeds of their religious scam. They were proud of the luxurious 5000-dollar dog house they bought for the backyard of their mansion.

Prosperity Gospel preachers developed clever marketing techniques to lure viewers to watch the television shows and send in their money. One of their favorite techniques owes more to literary studies than to religion and the Bible. Literary scholars talk about the concept of an offstage character. Offstage characters never appear before the audience on the stage. The audience learns about offstage characters through what other characters in the play say about them. Offstage characters are an effective literary and dramatic device. Offstage characters sometimes seem more real and colorful to the audience than other characters who actually appear onstage.

God is an offstage character in television talk shows for Bible believers. Though God never appears before the cameras, the hosts and guests on the show talk about God incessantly. Viewers get the impression that God helped produce the show, participates in the action and wants to help keep the show on the air.

God plays a leading role in the shows' televised fundraising campaigns. Performers create a scenario in which God is pacing nervously in Heaven. God is all ears, anxiously awaiting the latest news about the show's dire financial plight. God is worrying that viewers might not come through with enough money in time to save the show. But just as the creditors are banging on the studio door, God inspires generous donors to rescue the show with their last-minute donations.

I gather that this technique must work pretty effectively, for television preachers use it repeatedly. The show lives on because of a lively offstage character: God.

Don't get me wrong. I too would like to have a big bunch of money. I too have prayed for money at times, and sometimes it works. But my life experience suggests to me that God is more interested in my spiritual health than in my financial health. God is often more indirect with us than just sending a check. God sometimes uses a slow, subtle approach to make our dream come true.

## CHAPTER TEN

# God, my Daydream and my Daughter

One evening in the late spring of 1981 or 1982 I was swinging in my back porch swing in Charlottesville, Virginia. I already had two fine sons whom I loved dearly. I also always wanted a daughter but my wife had a hard time with her last pregnancy. So we decided it wasn't wise for her to get pregnant again.

That evening I had a daydream as I sat in the swing. I thought how great it would be to adopt a Native American daughter. I don't know where the daydream came from. The thought seemed to arise in my mind spontaneously and it was deep and heartfelt and poignant. I didn't send the daydream up as a prayer but

I dwelt on it for a long time that night. Afterward, I let the daydream go and never put any effort into making it come true.

Years passed by and my life changed completely. In 1993 I married my wife Cheryl. Cheryl had always wanted children but she had difficulties with fertility. We prayed to God to lead us to a baby to adopt. But several years went by with no luck.

In 1996, Cheryl and I went to New Mexico where I was to lecture on near-death experiences at a conference for helping professionals. We were sitting in the audience before my lecture listening to the previous presenter finish his lecture before I went to the podium. The lecturer indicated that now he would like to take questions from the audience.

A microphone had been set up in the middle aisle of the auditorium. The idea was that questioners would line up to await their turn at the microphone. Suddenly, Cheryl and I noticed that a Native American woman sitting next to me on my right seemed to be battling with herself. We realized that she obviously wanted to ask a question. But her body language betrayed that she was having trouble getting up the nerve. Cheryl tapped me on my arm and I took the woman - whose name is Christine - by her arm and escorted her to the microphone so she could ask her question.

Two years later, in 1998, Cheryl and I got to know a kind-hearted Mexican-American family. They were looking for a couple to adopt the baby their daughter would soon be having. Our son Carter was born on July 20, 1998 and Cheryl was there for the delivery. The obstetrician put Carter in Cheryl's arms and we soon got to know Carter as one of the sweetest people God ever put on the Earth. Of course, that sounds like a father talking but other people who know Carter well say the same thing. We settled in as loving parents of a loving son.

One day two years later, in August, 2000, the phone rang. When I answered it, Christine's voice greeted me cheerfully and asked "How are you doing?"

I answered that we were doing well and that we had adopted a baby. "Oh," Christine exclaimed, "I wish so much I had known you were looking!" She explained that she worked in the hospital on the Blackfeet Reservation. And she was always the first person to find out when a need for adoptive parents arose. I assured Christine that I had always wanted a daughter and asked her to please look for us.

Pretty soon thereafter, Christine called and told us that our daughter was on her way. Soon, Cheryl, Carter and I traveled to Montana to meet my daughter's birth mother and her family. Cheryl and I appeared before a Blackfeet judge who was to rule on our suitability as adoptive parents. The judge approved of us and a couple of months later Cheryl flew back to Montana to receive our daughter. Carol was born on November 5, 2000.

That was the advent of my daughter Carol who is one of the most interesting individuals I have ever had the pleasure of knowing. Christine, understanding her tribe as she does, told me in advance that my daughter was likely to be an assertive person. Christine remarked proudly that people often travel hundreds of miles out of their way to avoid having to drive through the Blackfeet Reservation. And I soon found out for myself that my dear daughter truly has a mind of her own.

When she was thirteen months old, for instance, Carol was sitting in my lap and I was letting her drink from a can of Diet Coke. From her first few days of life she always insisted on holding onto her baby bottle with her hands as we fed her. And that day as I sat in a chair she clasped the Diet Coke can with her hands as she drank from it. I tipped the can a little too high as I held it and Diet Coke splashed out of the can onto the front of her gown. She looked down at her gown and then looked at me straight in the eye with a stern gaze.

Carol jumped down from my lap and marched across the living room to the spot before the fireplace where she had left a little carton of grape juice. She picked up the carton and looked directly at me to be sure I saw her as she waved the carton back and forth before my eyes. Then she marched back across the living room, climbed back into my lap and shook grape juice all over the front of my shirt.

I like to walk and I pushed my children in a stroller when they were little. The boys enjoyed the walks but they lost interest in walking with me when they outgrew the stroller. Carol enjoyed the walks too but she wanted out of the stroller as soon as she could walk. She obviously wanted to walk along with me but like the overprotective father that I am, I wouldn't permit it. Then, when she was almost three years old she figured out how to unlock the seat belt and quickly climbed out of the stroller. We were about three quarters of a mile from home and I braced myself. I assumed that Carol's days of walking with me would be over. But to my surprise a determined expression appeared on her face. She gripped the handle of the stroller and pushed it all the way back home by herself. I walked along beside her, laughing most of the way. From that day forward for about ten years we walked together the same route of three to six miles.

Carol soon began to carry what she called her "nature bag" with her on our walks. She gathered plants and little animals and she had an uncanny ability to find birds' nests. One day she announced, "I'm going to find some birds' eggs." And within the next half mile she found three different species of birds' eggs.

I was astonished and I asked "How do you do that?" I saw her wheels turning as she tried her best to find the words to explain it to me. Finally, though, she gave up and brushed me off. She pointed to the other side of the road and said, "Just go over there and look."

During our walks, Carol liked to stop and sit and talk on an old wooden bridge about a mile from our house. One day when she was nine years old as we were sitting on the bridge she blurted out, "I don't like this place!"

From the way she said it I knew immediately she was talking about the world. In response I said something like "Ehhhh?" And she said, "Yeah! When you die you go up and be with God and He keeps you up there until all the people you knew while you're alive have died, and then He sends you back as another person."

I asked, "What makes you think so?"

She pointed with the fingertips of both her hands, pointing inwardly as if somewhere behind her eyes. And she said, "I just know, in my mind." And she continued immediately, "Yeah! I was with God and He pointed you out to me and He said, 'You gotta go down and be his daughter.' "

I asked, "How did you feel about that?"

She exclaimed, "Oh, I didn't wanna do it. I wanted to stay with my God-dee."

Then she thrust both her hands out in front of her, twice, in a strong, pushing motion. And as she did she said, "But He pushed me down to be your daughter."

She did add, though, that she was glad she came anyway.

I didn't ask her any more questions because I didn't want to put anything in her mind. Perhaps partly because of that, Carol still remembers this and once in a while she brings it up herself. Occasionally, she says, "I wonder why they pushed me out of that light."

She has continued to wonder that throughout her life. She has had her share of emotional troubles and a couple of stormy relationships. Like me, she knows that life is not all sweetness and light. God's educational strategy includes some suffering, discontent and strife.

Raising a Native American daughter turned out to present challenges I had not anticipated. Carol learned to read before she went to school and she read a lot of books about Pocahontas. One day when she was six years old she looked directly at Cheryl and me. "Were your people English?" she asked. When we acknowledged that they were, Carol said, "Your people hurt my people."

When she became a teenager, true to that step of

development, she would get irritated at Cheryl and me from time to time. When she did she would often moan and say, "Oh, I'm just gonna go back and live on my reservation." When I told Christine about that, she laughed and said, "Well I suspect that when she got out here she would just turn around and head back home."

One day when she was eleven years old Carol decided she wanted to find a snail. So we set out on our three mile walk searching for a snail. Along the way we looked everywhere we could think of. We looked under the old wooden bridge, along the banks of a creek and beneath bushes that lined the side of the road. But we searched to no avail.

As we headed back home, Carol walked a few paces behind me. We were about a half mile from home when I heard a shout of joy from behind me. I turned around and saw that Carol had found a little snail about a quarter of an inch in diameter. The snail was exactly the same dark color as the soil alongside the road. She picked the snail up from the dirt and held it gently between the tips of her forefinger and thumb.

She held the snail up and showed it to me and she said, "God makes your dream come true."

When Carol said that, my mind went back to the night I was sitting in my back porch swing in Charlottesville. I thought of the daydream I had that night and of the poignant feelings I had. And I thought, "God certainly does."

My relationship with my daughter has been a highlight of my life. One of many important things she has taught me is that God watches over us in ways mysterious. We need to listen carefully and attentively to hear what God might be saying to us. God's language is immeasurably more subtle, perceptive, indirect, thought-provoking, insightful, allusive and penetrating than is human language.

That brings us to the twelfth of my thoughts about God that make up this book. Many insist that their religion's holy scriptures are purely literal in meaning and contain the literal truth about God. Literalism is another human personality quirk that often blocks a heartfelt relationship with God.

Literal meaning was definitely not stamped into the nature of reality at the beginning of time. Insisting on literal meaning in the Bible, for instance, is an anachronism. Plato and other Greek philosophers constructed the concept of literal meaning during the classical period when they were developing logic. I can't imagine that in talking to us God worries about conforming to Greek philosophers' logical principals about literal meaning. This is another illuminating case where having a good sense of humor comes in handy when we are thinking about religious doctrines. The image of an uptight Bible believer trying to dictate that God must stick to literal meanings would be outrageous, if it weren't so funny.

God doesn't always make perfect sense. God speaks to us in all sorts of imaginative language that defies literal meaning - including nonsense. Nonsense is meaningless, unintelligible language that occurs mostly in literature - especially children's literature -

but which also often has spiritual significance. And cultivating a lively sense of nonsense is a proven way of getting closer to God.

## CHAPTER ELEVEN

# God and Dr. Seuss

God's people love nonsense. Dr. Seuss's books of nonsense for children have sold more than 600 million copies all around the world. Lewis Carroll's classic nineteenth century works of children's nonsense - *Alice in Wonderland* and *Through the Looking Glass* - continue to entertain multitudes of readers worldwide. And nonsense is for adults, too.

Angelic singers Ella Fitzgerald's and Louis Armstrong's jazz songs consisted of improvised nonsense syllables. Their performances transported enthralled listeners to blissful, almost otherworldly states of consciousness. Doo-wop songs that were popular throughout the 1950's used nonsense as the main line or for harmony. Doo-wop songs combined nonsense with meaningful words into a unified whole. Doo-wop songs can induce trance-like states of consciousness.

Consciousness-raising shaman songs were constructed much like doo-wop songs. Shaman songs were made up of nonsense syllables and meaningless refrains put together with elements of meaningful and intelligible language. Singing these songs transported shamans into ecstatic states of awareness that they experienced as crossing over into the spirit world. This is only one of a host of spiritual and religious practices that use nonsense for transforming consciousness. Nonsense plainly has a transcendent dimension.

God sometimes talks nonsense to send messages to us straight across boundaries that separate the earthly from the heavenly spheres of reality. That happened to my wife Cheryl, my adopted son Carter and me. God bound us together in a heavenly pact of nonsense.

Carter was born on July 20, 1998 in Kerrville,

Texas. He was discharged from the hospital three days later and we went to a local restaurant with Carter's birth family. Carter's birth mother, her father and mother, Cheryl, Carter in his baby carrier and I sat together and talked during lunch. The gist of the conversation was that Carter will always know his birth family. We agreed that in the fullness of time we would be reunited.

Amidst our conversation, I noticed a wooden placard with a nonsensical message on the restaurant wall. The message reflected exactly what we were saying. For the placard said:

CLOSED

> I have gone out to find
> myself. If I should
> arrive before I return,
> please hold me till I
> come back.

Carter's birth family did hold him until we got together again, too. In April, 2011, the whole family visited Cheryl, Carter, my daughter Carol and me in our home and spent a week with us. And Carter still keeps in touch with his birth family.

The nonsensical words on the placard accurately described and foretold what happened in life. So nonsense sometimes conveys a spiritual meaning between different dimensions of life and levels of consciousness. Carter's cross-dimensional communication was a deeply meaningful spiritual experience in my life.

At first, the idea of using nonsense for communicating with God may seem shocking and counterintuitive. Yet upon reflection we easily remember that nonsense is an ancient, still thriving practice for carrying on a living relationship with God. Glossolalia, or speaking in unknown tongues, is associated with the Christian faith, for the most part. However, it is also practiced in some other religious and spiritual traditions.

Linguistically, glossolalia is the spontaneous utterance of a stream of nonsense syllables drawn from the speaker's own language. The nonsense syllables are strung together in such a way that there are no actual words and no grammatical structure. You don't need to participate in a church service or be in an ecstatic state to speak in unknown tongues. You can just let go of your inhibitions and spontaneously utter nonsense syllables. Continuing the practice for a while brings about an uplifting ecstatic or mystical experience. I tried glossolalia myself and was awed by the inspiring, unifying state of consciousness it created. I can easily imagine that such an uplifted state could open someone to an experiential encounter with God.

Nonsense also enters into central theological concepts of various religions. Christianity's doctrine of the Trinity is a case in point. According to the Trinity, God is one single person in three persons: the Father, the Son, and the Holy Ghost. Though the doctrine is vital to many believers, in reality the Trinity has no intelligible meaning. One and three are distinct numbers and to say that one is identical to three is unintelligible nonsense. The Trinity is nonsense because it breaks the rules of arithmetic and destroys the very meanings of numbers.

As a theological doctrine, the Trinity is nonsense. In medieval times, though, the Trinity was not so much a doctrine as a kind of logico-spiritual mental exercise. Wrestling with the perplexities of the Trinity by thinking about it logically was a way of contemplating the identity of God. The idea was to generate insights into the nature of God by thinking rigorously and logically about the paradoxes of the Trinity.

In that respect, the Trinity bears some resemblances to Zen Buddhism's Koans. Koans include some nonsensical and unintelligible questions such as "What is the sound of one hand clapping?" A Zen master chooses an appropriate Koan to assign to a student. The student tries at first to answer the illogical questions by applying logical reasoning. That won't work, though, and eventually the futile task breaks the student's mind through into transcendent states that lie beyond logic and reasoning.

Excessive preoccupation with logic and reason can keep us distant from God. Nonsense can break down fixation on logic and reason and move us closer to God. The mind we have does not get us far toward comprehending God. But we can empower our minds to think logically about unintelligible nonsense. And that leads us a little closer toward comprehending God. Every little advance in consciousness helps. That can help us be more amenable and open to a relationship with God.

In my mind, learning to love within a personal relationship with God is the defining purpose of life. Still, many people feel a need to think as deeply as they can about God. They try logical reasoning as a path toward comprehending the Supreme Being. Some great thinkers who took that path ultimately arrived at a barrier of unintelligibility. They came to see that from the standpoint of literal meaning, talk about God is nonsensical.

G.C. Lichtenberg (1742-1799), a German philosopher and scientist, was a pioneer of this kind of reflection. He observed that whichever way we turn, we eventually come up against something that is unintelligible and nonsensical. Lichtenberg was fascinated by nonsense which he generally thought of as something positive and valuable. He commented that trying to make sense of incomprehensible nonsense often sparks valuable new ideas. And Lichtenberg was the first person to state what is known today as the incommensurability principle. The principle concerns potential difficulties of communicating with vastly advanced extraterrestrial civilizations, for instance. Suppose, Lichtenberg said, that a superior intelligence tried to tell us something. Lichtenberg said that what the superior intelligence said would sound to us like "2 times 2 equals 13."

Lichtenberg pointed out that many people's idea of God is a personification of unintelligibility and nonsense. For instance, many characterize God as omniscient, omnipotent and omnipresent. Those are impressive words. Even so, what real sense can any of us have of the meanings of the concepts that lie behind them? If we are to be honest, we must admit that we cannot even imagine omniscience, omnipotence and omnipresence. Yet we can have a relationship with God.

Lichtenberg was fond of bringing out paradoxes in our idea of God. He once said, "I thank God that He lets me be an atheist." Lichtenberg's keen appreciation of nonsense helped inspire two major twentieth century movements in art and philosophy - surrealism and analytic philosophy.

Logical positivism - an early movement of analytic philosophers - originated in Europe in about 1915. Logical positivists considered scientific method to be the hallmark of rational thought. They dismissed anything that was not verifiable as meaningless nonsense, including all talk about God and ethical ideals. A.J. Ayer, a renowned proponent of logical positivism, wrote a book entitled *Language, Truth and Logic*. In his book, Ayer wrote, "that there is no possibility of demonstrating the existence of a god." However, Ayer went on to add, "If the assertion that there is a god is nonsensical, then the atheist's assertion that there is no god is equally nonsensical."

Traditionally, that kind of criticism has been viewed as the worst case scenario for the idea of God. Indeed, many even consider that criticism to be a decisive reason for dismissing God. However, such critics are entirely mistaken.

The idea of God is nonsense. At first, that statement sounds like an insult. Or, the statement could be another way of saying that God does not exist. Actually, however, neither of those analyses bears scrutiny.

"The idea of God is nonsense" is a statement about the limits of the human mind. Calling the idea of God unintelligible nonsense is a reminder that the mind cannot comprehend God. The statement means that God transcends all the conceptual systems that the intellect may use to make sense or reality. But isn't that exactly what reflective people have always thought about God in the first place?

Attempts to comprehend God with logic and

reason are futile. That is, our intellectual mind cannot corral God within concepts and abstractions. Embracing nonsense as a valid dimension of thought and communication helps ease the way to cherishing God's companionship. Here again we see that what we need to do is concentrate on our personal relationships with God.

# CHAPTER TWELVE

# God and the Afterlife

God is coming soon. That thought often fills the minds of terminally ill people. They frequently look back and reflect on how quickly their lives had seemed to pass by. In the process of dying, time itself seems to collapse. On their deathbeds, people compare life to the blinking of an eye.

Whoever we are, wherever we are, however old or young we are, God is coming soon. That thought occupies the minds of dying people. Furthermore, it is a good thought for all of us to keep constantly on our minds. We will be with God soon.

End-of-life reflections raise questions concerning life after death. How is God connected to the mystery of an afterlife? A few thinkers about religion theorize that people invented the idea of God to guarantee themselves a life after death. In other words, people dreamed up God who then would supposedly provide a place where they could continue personal consciousness beyond death. These theorists of religion maintain that if people knew for certain that there is no afterlife, they would throw God away, too.

I disagree with those thinkers' theory and attitude. I found God many years before I came to the jarring realization that, yes, there is a life beyond death. For all I knew, God had something else in mind for us than continuing self-awareness after death.

Of course, I talked to thousands of sincere people about their near-death experiences. Their accounts inspired me with an ideal of learning to love others. However, no logical method leads securely from those accounts to a sound conclusion that there is an afterlife. Even so, no logical method leads securely to the opposite conclusion, either. I simply had no idea whether or not there is an afterlife.

Life after death may well be the biggest question of human existence. Life after death is a serious question that deserves serious rational investigation. We should get real about this pivotal mystery of life. Intellectual honesty requires us to wrestle bravely with the strongest objections and gravest difficulties. Otherwise, we would be deceiving ourselves.

In reality, though, the standard objection raised in popular debates about near-death experiences is not very formidable. Many object that experiences like those are caused by oxygen deprivation to the brain. However, the occurrence of shared death experiences undermines that objection. Shared death experiences occur among bystanders at the death of some other person. The bystanders themselves are not ill or injured. Yet as the other person dies, the bystanders enter into transcendent states of consciousness. The bystanders report that they got out of their bodies and accompanied the dying person part way toward the light. In fact, bystanders report all the familiar elements of near-death experiences. Therefore, some other factor or factors than oxygen deprivation to the brain must be present to account for transcendent experiences of the dying. In sum, shared death experiences have all the same elements as near-death experiences. Yet people who have shared death experiences do not have a compromised oxygen supply to their brains.

"Oxygen deprivation to the brain" is a flash-in-the-pan, a slogan people use to avoid thinking about tough philosophical problems. Still, the oxygen deprivation theory is unlikely to go away anytime soon. For the theory has a great deal of entertainment value. Many people have fun debating about near-death experiences as a kind of hobby. They are attached to the traditional format of debate that involves talking about oxygen deprivation to the brain.

The oxygen deprivation theory also involves a powerful comfort factor. Some devotees of the subject prefer to keep on treading the well-worn path. For them, near-death experiences and the prospect of an afterlife are a strange, potentially scary, unsettling territory. Some may cling consciously or unconsciously to the notion of oxygen deprivation. That may help them avoid facing the possibility of a higher, more inclusive sphere of reality beyond our current knowledge.

Even so, proving that near-death experiences are not caused by oxygen deprivation still does not prove life after death. We need to go deeper to investigate that question rigorously. We need to venture out into a new way of thinking about God, transcendent experiences of the dying, and life after death.

In this life, many people view God through the lens of their religious beliefs. In contrast, people often meet God directly and personally during their near-death experiences. They tell us that a vivid sense of the immediacy of God fills the next life. God's presence is manifest and direct in the world beyond. Hence, learning more about the afterlife may bring us closer to God.

To get there, we need to remove four major obstacles that impede rigorous rational inquiry into the afterlife. Four great philosophers – Plato, David Hume, A. J. Ayer, and William James – pinpointed the crucial difficulties. These philosophers identified four interrelated problems that, together, prevent effective logical thinking about life after death.

We will first examine the four problems separately. We will look at how the four problems are related to near-death experiences and life after death. Then, we will put the four problems together and solve them all in one fell swoop.

Furthermore, this solution will be accessible to everyone. That is, anyone will be able to verify and confirm the solution. Everyone will be able to think the solution through for themselves in their own minds and prove it to their own satisfaction.

## Plato's Narrative/Concept Problem

Plato (428-348 BCE) wrote the first systematic analysis of problems that constrain attempts at rational proof of an afterlife. His dialogue *Phaedo* laid the groundwork for all subsequent rational investigations of this mystery. *Phaedo* is also a great work of literature. The dialogue recounts the final thoughts of Plato's teacher Socrates before he was executed by hemlock poisoning. The early Church Fathers derived much of the Christian theology of the afterlife from Plato's *Phaedo*.

In the dialogue, Plato identified what I call the narrative/concept problem. Specifically, Plato pointed out that we have only an obscure, imprecise notion of life after death. Therefore, he said, we always need some sort of story, or narrative, just to get discussion of the question started.

The Greeks had the same sorts of stories about the afterlife that we still have today. Plato and other Greek philosophers studied reports of near-death experiences by people who recovered after almost dying. Plato was inspired and encouraged by these stories just as people are inspired and encouraged by them today.

The trouble is, Plato said, that even a million of these stories would not add up to rational proof of an afterlife. In addition, Plato said, we need some set of concepts that logically connect the stories to the conclusion that there is life after death. Without such concepts, the yearning for rational support is always left unsatisfied. The narrative/concept problem still besets people who are fascinated by near-death experiences and the question of a life beyond death.

Many people are enthralled and consoled by stories of near-death experiences. However, the resulting thrill and consolation are not permanent. Pretty soon, the uplifting spell the story casts fades away. Then, doubts and worries about death resurface. The person wants to hear another inspiring story to be thrilled and consoled once again. For there are no concepts that enable anyone to make rational sense of near-death experiences in relation to life after death.

I have known many people who get trapped in that endless cycle. They got addicted to enthralling stories of near-death experiences. Hearing one story comforted them temporarily, but created an appetite for hearing more stories. The longing for rational proof thereby gets thwarted.

How can we break the cycle? We need concepts that logically connect the stories to the statement that there is an afterlife. However, virtually everyone loves enthralling and comforting stories. In contrast, though, relatively few people love thinking about concepts. I know many people who would gladly sit still for hours listening to stories of near-death experiences. Yet if you try to explain abstract concepts to them they quickly get bored and roll their eyes up into their heads. Hence, they set themselves up for a permanent, dissatisfied state of longing and yearning. Eventually, a foray into conceptual thinking is necessary for putting to rest the longing for rational proof of an afterlife.

When Plato wrote *Phaedo*, he did the best he could with concepts that were then available. At that time, there was no such thing as logic as we know it. That is, there was not a standard code of rules for governing logical reasoning. Plato's student Aristotle codified the rules of logical reasoning we use today. Aristotle's logic has been spectacularly successful. We use his logic for scholarly and scientific purposes as well as reasoning about the problems of everyday life.

Hence, you might well expect that Aristotle's logic would be the key to rational proof of an afterlife. However, that turned out not to be true. Aristotle's logic is just as incompetent to prove an afterlife as Plato's more limited concepts were. That brings us to the second major problem that constrains rational investigation of life after death.

## Hume's Incomprehensibility Problem

David Hume (1711-1776) was a Scottish philosopher whose analyses of causation and inductive reasoning helped shape the scientific mind. For instance, Hume's works strongly impressed and influenced Albert Einstein. Hume also propounded a revelatory insight into the difficulty of rational proof of life after death.

Hume wrote:

"By the mere light of reason, it seems difficult to prove the immortality of the soul... Some new species of logic is requisite for that purpose; and some new faculties of the mind, that they may enable us to comprehend that logic."

Hume's blunt, incisive statement is correct. In reality, the logic we have and the mind we have cannot prove life after death. Hume also implied that it is impossible for us to come up with the required new species of logic and new faculties of the mind. After all, Aristotle's logic has served us well for centuries. Coming up with some new code of logic may seem out of the question. Besides, we think we know our own minds very well. The idea that we might discover some new, previously unknown capacities of the mind seems fanciful at best.

Hume was right when he insisted that the logic and the mind we have are inadequate for proving an afterlife. However, Hume was wrong when he implied that it is impossible to fix this problem. In fact, we can devise a suitable new system of logical principles.

Furthermore, learning this new system of logic happens to awaken suitable new capacities of the mind. Then, we can use this new logic and new mental capacities to make a major breakthrough in the rigorous rational investigation of life after death.

To see why and how we need to move on and consider the work of some later philosophers. Hume did not specify exactly why our current logic is incapable of proving life after death. In the twentieth century, some of Hume's successors filled in that detail.

## Ayer's Unintelligibility Problem

A.J. Ayer (1910-1989) was an early proponent of analytic philosophy, the method of thinking that dominates the field today. Analytic philosophers continued in the tradition of Hume, focusing on careful logical reasoning and paying close attention to the meanings of words. Analytic philosophers realized that upon close analysis many traditional philosophical theories are actually meaningless and unintelligible, or nonsensical.

Life after death is one of the old, philosophical problems that some analytic philosophers dismissed as unintelligible nonsense. For instance, Ayer claimed that the notion of life after death is self-contradictory. In his classic book *Language, Truth and Logic* (1936), Ayer said "Whereas it is permissible, in our language, to speak of a man as surviving a complete loss of memory, or a complete change of character, it is self-contradictory to speak of a man as surviving the annihilation of his body."

Certainly, the words "life after death" may stir up appealing images and warm fuzzy feelings in our minds. However, when we subject the words to careful logical scrutiny we find that they do not have a clear meaning. In other words, all talk about life after death is unintelligible nonsense. Reflecting on near-death experiences helps confirm this.

People say that their near-death experiences did not take place in time but in a transcendent realm beyond time. Furthermore, they say that their experiences did not take place in space as we know it.

Yet, they tell us that they got out of their bodies and went through a tunnel into a bright, comforting, loving light. In that light, they met deceased loved ones and saw their lives pass by in review. Then, they returned to their bodies and came back to life.

That kind of account is obviously a travel narrative, but they already told us that their experiences were not in time or space. However, a travel narrative, by definition, recounts a passage from one place to another place during a period of time. Accordingly, stories of near-death experiences are nonsensical travel narratives.

Nonsense laid out in the format of a travel story can create a curious sense of motion in the mind. You can experience this for yourself by introspecting as you read the nonsensical sentence that follows.

Nine shining smenaters troddled blustfully from the central treshnut on God's mathematical island to life's whirling zone of trenation.

The sentence is meaningless, unintelligible nonsense. Yet reading and pondering it reveals that the sentence stirs garbled mental images and vague semi-thoughts in the mind. The mind is not blank when we read meaningless nonsense. Instead, we experience an active process as the mind tries to make sense of the sentence. We get a vague sense of something undefined going from one place to another. That is how the mind tries to process stories of near-death experiences, because they are also nonsensical travel narratives.

When we read or hear somebody's story of their near-death experiences, we are aware of an odd, inner sense of motion. Somehow it feels like something in the mind moves, though not through physical space. The sense of mental motion seems to convey hearers' or readers' thoughts from this world to another realm beyond death.

This is just what we would expect in light of what

we already learned about nonsense. In chapter 11, we saw that nonsense is a vital force in spiritual life. Speaking in unknown tongues, or glossolalia, and Zen Buddhist koans, use nonsense to bring about ecstatic states and experiences of spiritual consciousness. Nonsense connects us to spiritual states that seemingly transcend the ordinary sphere of reality. Similarly, hearing nonsensical travel narratives of near-death experiences can bring about an uplifting spiritual state of the conscious mind. That is understandable, given our previous knowledge about the valuable spiritual effects of nonsense.

All this reveals what Hume's "new species of logic" needs to be. Namely, we need a logic of nonsense for genuinely rational investigation of the afterlife. And a logic of nonsense sounds like an impossible dream. In fact, though, it is an accomplished reality. I developed such a logic during my career as a philosophy professor and psychiatrist.

I gathered all my research into a semester-length course on nonsense and taught it numerous times at several universities. In addition, I taught seminars on nonsense for dozens of professional organizations. My courses and seminars covered literary, psychological, medical, scientific, spiritual, and commercial implications and applications of unintelligible nonsense. I created written, mental exercises concerning nonsense for students and participants in my university courses and professional seminars.

In working on those exercises, students used mental powers they had never before realized they possessed. They found that they can distinguish among many different types of nonsense. They also realized that they can discern the distinctive structural patterns of different types of nonsense. They even found that they can create their own original examples of different types of nonsense. Students reported they felt the wheels of their minds turning in a new way. When they shifted from creating one type of nonsense to creating some other type they discovered a new type of cognitive process within their minds.

These newfound capacities turn out to be Hume's

"new faculties of the mind" required for rational investigation of the afterlife. My logic of nonsense, together with these new mental capacities, supports a revolutionary breakthrough in research. For we can now resolve the fourth major problem that holds back rational investigation of life after death.

## James's Ineffability Problem

William James (1842-1910), an eminent American philosopher, was a pioneer in the field of psychology. His book *Varieties of Religious Experience* (1902) includes a brilliant analysis of mystical experiences. James observed that ineffability is the most conspicuous characteristic of mystical experiences. That is, people who report mystical experiences say that there is no way to describe them or adequately put them into words.

In that respect, near-death experiences are a mystical state of consciousness. For the most common thing people say about their near-death experiences is that there is no way to describe their experiences in words. However articulate or well-educated they are, or however many languages they speak, people say that their near-death experiences are indescribable or ineffable.

James ineffability problem helps explain why accounts of near-death experiences must be nonsensical. Profound near-death experiences are ineffable and indescribable. Therefore, people who want to talk at all about their near-death experiences are obliged to talk nonsense about them. No ordinary meaningful words are adequate. Hence, people are forced to try and convey a sense of what their experiences were like by using unintelligible, nonsensical language instead.

That is one aspect of what gives stories of near-death experiences their power to enthrall the mind. The stories exert their awesome mental and spiritual effects partly because they are nonsense and partly because they are structured like a travel narrative. Somewhat paradoxically, people often pay closer attention to nonsense than they do to ordinary, meaningful, language.

People's travel narratives of their near-death experiences are nonsense, but they communicate anyway. Three considerations show that this paradox is true. First, many people from many different backgrounds report personal near-death experiences. They independently selected the nonsensical travel narrative format to recount their experiences. Hence, a nonsense travel narrative must somehow be appropriate for conveying some shared characteristic or quality of near-death experiences.

Secondly, in the 1970's I conducted numerous group discussions among people who reported near-death experiences. None of the individuals who participated had ever before recounted their experiences in a group setting. None of them had ever met anyone else with such an experience. And in almost every case, I was the only person with whom they had previously shared their experience.

Participants in these discussions showed a great

deal of surprise, delight and relief when they heard others recount personal near-death experiences. Up to that point, many participants felt alone in having their experiences. In the group settings, the nonsense travel narrative format clearly facilitated mutual comprehension among the participants.

Thirdly, someone may read or hear accounts of near-death experiences before having their own experience at a later time. And when they do, they may recognize what is happening to them as a near-death experience, based on their knowledge of the earlier accounts. I first heard someone describe this in the summer of 1979, in New Jersey.

A group had invited me to lecture and after the event they had a backyard barbeque. My hostess told me that she had read my book *Life After Life* shortly after it was published in 1975. She said that about a year before the barbeque she underwent gall bladder surgery, suffered a cardiac arrest and was successfully revived. During her near-death experience, she thought "This is just like the book".

Since then, I heard quite a few people describe that same thing. People cast their personal near-death experiences in the form of nonsensical travel narratives. Some other individual may then learn about near-death experiences from those nonsensical narratives. Learning in that way enables that individual to recognize a subsequent personal transformation of consciousness as a near-death experience. Accordingly, unintelligible nonsense facilitated the learning and transmission of information about a spiritual state of consciousness.

The three considerations above catch nonsense amidst a transitional process. What was previously unintelligible nonsense is gradually becoming public knowledge about near-death experiences. To summarize, then, nonsense can sometimes effectively communicate knowledge about transcendent experiences that are ineffable, or indescribable.

Furthermore, most people love travel stories. Hence, casting accounts of near-death experiences in that format helps ground them in the familiar.

We have now brought together all the knowledge we need to make a great leap forward. My method for imparting logical principles is key to better rational comprehension of the afterlife. The process implants principles of nonsense and unintelligibility permanently in the mind. Completing the process prepares someone's mind to get a firmer cognitive hold on a subsequent near-death experience. That constitutes a way around the ineffability problem.

During the near-death experience, the conscious mind crosses over into a transcendent realm. People who absorb principles of the logic of nonsense can carry those principles when they cross to the next life. That empowers the mind to interact cognitively with a near-death experience in a new, more effective way. That will influence how a person puts their experience into words, upon being revived. In other words, learning the logic of nonsense will affect how someone recounts their near-death experience in the future. In effect, advance knowledge of logical principles of nonsense alleviates the problem of ineffability.

This has already happened. A renowned artist and scientist participated in one of my nonsense seminars. Several years later he almost died from a severe case of influenza. During his ordeal he underwent three cardiac arrests and had profound near-death experiences. He said that when he was on the other side his mind went back to the nonsense seminar. From that vantage point, he realized why knowledge of principles of nonsense is necessary for comprehending how the next life is related to this life.

This man's reports of his near-death experiences differ considerably from the familiar travel narrative accounts. Instead he recounted his near-death experiences as direct conversations with God. He said that God showed him a "holographic video" of his life and discussed his life with him.

As time passes, more people who understand logical principles of nonsense will happen to have their own near-death experiences. Their accounts will differ from the familiar accounts that we already have. Existing accounts represent the afterlife as viewed solely through the lens of Aristotelian logic. The forthcoming accounts will represent the afterlife as viewed through the lens of Aristotelian logic supplemented and strengthened by the logic of nonsense. I know there will be differences, but obviously, I don't know yet what the exact differences will be. That is part of what makes this study exciting, and I am confident we will find out pretty soon. Then, comparing the new accounts with the existing accounts will give us valuable information. The two different types of accounts will represent the afterlife from two different angles. Hence, we will be able to see how the afterlife looks from two different vantage points. We will be able to get a more precise fix on the next life by a kind of mental triangulation.

A rational proof of life after death will not come from a single individual working alone. Nor will a proof come from a small team of dedicated researchers. Instead, many people need to participate in a large collective research project. Together, we can step across the mental and logical frontier that separates this life from the life hereafter. I am proposing a collective study of near-death experiences and the afterlife in which anyone can participate. My study first prepares participants' minds to think with a new logic about life after death; then, they will be able to describe their subsequent near-death experiences utilizing the tools they have learned.

My book *Making Sense of Nonsense* (Llewellyn Publications, 2020) brings all my research together in a single volume. The book also includes the exercises that were an integral part of my courses and seminars. *Making Sense of Nonsense* also serves as a guidebook for readers participating in my collective study of near-death experiences and life after death.

You can join the collective study by reading the book and completing the exercises. That will reformat your mind and enable you to think logically about things that are unintelligible and nonsensical. This process has many practical benefits. Learning the logic of nonsense improves critical and analytical reasoning and inspires creative thinking. Knowing the logic of nonsense is highly useful for writers, teachers, psychologists, physicians, advertisers and professionals in numerous other fields.

The process also prepares you to be a better observer and investigator of any near-death experience you might have in the future. Principles of nonsense would enable you to realize that a travel narrative of your experience would be unintelligible. You would shift your account away from that format to make it more intelligible to others. Ultimately, we would begin to formulate new publicly understandable concepts and vocabulary for the talking about such experiences. Together, we could enlighten humankind on the greatest, deepest mystery of life.

My readers have a right to know what I think about the prospect of a life beyond death. What is my personal stance toward the afterlife in light of my several decades of research? I think that a dying individual's personal consciousness emerges from the physical world and finds itself in a larger, more inclusive sphere of reality. In that larger sphere, personal consciousness no longer orients itself by where in space it is or by what time it is. Instead, in that other sphere, there is a different coordinate system. By that system, personal consciousness appears to orient itself by love and by information or knowledge. I can condense and summarize the above by that I think there is a life after death.

I could not and would not make that statement in a void. That is, I would not make the statement unless there were publicly confirmable and understandable concepts that explain and support the statement. Specifically, the logic of nonsense forms the conceptual background of my statement. Others may agree or disagree with my judgement that there is life after death. The logic of nonsense is a common reference point by which such agreements or disagreements can be judged or mediated. And I claim that the logic of nonsense will prove superior to ordinary logic for mediating such controversies.

This kind of collective research project marks a fork in the road with respect to rational inquiry into the afterlife. From this point onward progress requires a shift in thinking. We need to supplement story-based thinking by integrating it with concept-based thinking. And we can do this by learning and absorbing rational principles for thinking logically about unintelligible nonsense.

I am confident that this research will yield valuable results. Eventually, this collective study of near-death experiences will lead to better rational comprehension of life after death. Yet rational comprehension of the afterlife will still leave us a long way from rational comprehension of God. God subsumes reason but reason cannot subsume God.

God is a far greater and deeper mystery than life after death. Just as God is bigger than the Bible and God is bigger than existence itself, God far surpasses the life beyond death. But additional rational insight into near-death experiences and life after death might also give us more insight into God.

A wondrous, comforting picture of God emerges from people's stories of near-death experiences. They reveal God's nature as a wise, loving companion and counsellor and a compassionate educator. God is definitely someone you would want to be with forever, judging from people's stories of their near-death experiences.

God's presence and accessibility to us are steeped in paradox. God transcends this life. Yet God is also present and accessible to us in this life. God even transcends the next life. Yet studies of near-death experiences make it seem that God is somehow more immediately present and more directly accessible in the next life. Hopefully, our collective study of near-death experiences might someday make God's presence more immediate in this world.

In the meantime, seek a richer, fuller relationship with God. Don't feel that you have to be formal, solemn, stilted or ceremonial around God. Laugh and have a good time. Open up, relax, pray, surrender and talk things over with God as though you were talking to an old friend. Go to God with your joys and with your sorrows. Try it for a while; make it a regular practice. Observe, reflect and watch what happens. Perhaps nothing will; perhaps everything will. Either way, you will be enlightened.

## AFTERWORD

Learning about God is a process that goes on throughout this life and into the next life. This book gathers together what I learned about God from people's stories of their near-death experiences and from my personal spiritual encounters.

THE END

This is a good place to recap my thirteen thoughts about God:

(1)     God is bigger than the *Bible*.

(2)     God is greater than existence itself.

(3)     God participates in our relationships with other people.

(4)     God loves us more than we love God.

(5)     God loves watching our life stories.

(6)     God is not interested in justice.

(7)     God does not care whether or not we join a religion.

(8)     God is no excuse for ignorance.

(9)     God continually creates everything.

(10)    God is not an automated teller machine.

(11)    God makes your dream come true.

(12)    God does not always make perfect sense.

(13)    God transcends the afterlife.

Made in the USA
Columbia, SC
17 February 2025

53925101R00102